Wit's End

About the Endpapers

Seated around the table are (clockwise):
Robert Sherwood, Dorothy Parker,
Robert Benchley, Alexander Wooll-
cott, Heywood Broun, Marc Connelly,
Franklin P. Adams, Edna Ferber, and
George S. Kaufman. At table in left
background are Lynn Fontanne and
Alfred Lunt, with Frank Crowninshield
standing. In background at right is
Frank Case, owner of the Algonquin
Hotel.

This drawing by Al Hirschfeld has
been used with the kind permission of
Horizon magazine and Mr. Hirschfeld.

Wit's End

The Best of the Brilliant Humour of
the Celebrated 'Round Table'
('The Vicious Circle of Wit') at the
Algonquin Hotel, New York

Edited by
Robert E. Drennan

Leslie Frewin of London

First published in Great Britain in 1973 by
Leslie Frewin Publishers Limited,
Five Goodwin's Court, St. Martin's Lane,
London, WC2N 4LL.
This book is reproduced Lithographically by
Biddles of Guildford
and bound by R. J. Acford, Industrial Estate, Chichester, England
World Rights Reserved

ISBN 0 85632 063 3

To the Memory of T.A.D. and E.C.U.,
Connecticut Wits

Acknowledgments

The editor wishes to thank the following for permission to reprint the material included in this book:

Ring Lardner, Jr., for selections from *Say It With Oil* by Ring Lardner, published by Doubleday & Co., copyright 1923 by G. H. Doran Co., and from *The Ring Lardner Reader*, published by Charles Scribner's Sons, copyright 1963.

The Viking Press, Inc., for *The Letters of Alexander Woollcott*, edited by Beatrice Kaufman and Joseph Hennessey, copyright 1944.

American Heritage Publishing Co., Inc., for Al Hirschfeld's drawing of the Round Table group which appeared originally in *Horizon* magazine, 1962.

Bennett Cerf for access to his several published collections of anecdotes by and about various Round Table figures.

Special thanks also to the Misses Jamey Frucht, Brenda Fisher, and Jacqueline Pierce for secretarial assistance, and to Michael MacRae for whatever it was that he contributed.

Finally, sincere thanks to A. A. Anspach of the Algonquin Hotel for his many gracious services (editorial suggestions included!) during the making of this book.

Contents

Wit's End

Cast of Characters

Harpo Marx, Paul Robeson, Noël Coward, Alfred Lunt
—*theatrical stars*
Margalo Gilmore, Peggy Wood, Tallulah Bankhead,
Lynn Fontanne—*actresses*
Beatrice Kaufman—*Mrs. George S.*
Charles MacArthur—*humorist and playwright*

PLACE

New York City. The Algonquin Hotel's Rose Room,
known for its patrician charm and sparkling conversation.

TIME

The 1920s, a period in American history remembered
for its gaiety, lawlessness, prosperity. A time of relief,
following "the war to end all wars"; significant value-
changes—urbanity, sophistication, literacy, taste, fashion replacing the old frontier spirit, the call of adventure
and the unknown; Prohibition, bootlegging, speakeasies
—all goals immediate (if not quite real).

In 1920, when Frank Case, owner of the Algonquin
Hotel, installed a large round table in the hotel's Rose
Room for the apparent purpose of catering to a group of
young, unknown literati, no one—least of all the group
itself—presumed so much as to attach any historical sig-
nificance to the gesture. Case himself would have argued
that the move was simply practical; the young men and

women, for better or worse, had chosen the Algonquin as their favorite luncheon place, originally meeting in the Oak Room and then migrating to the Rose Room, where, until they were given their special table, complete with private waiter and free relish trays, their expanding group overflowed daily into the aisles. The Algonquin became in fact as well as in spirit the focal point of much of the group's activity. A typical incident was the time *New Yorker* editor Harold Ross broke a dinner engagement with Aleck Woollcott (without telling him why) so that he could go to the theater with playwright Marc Connelly. Connelly and Ross made the mistake of dining at the Algonquin, where they were spotted by Woollcott, who obviously took it as a personal insult. Later that night Woollcott received the following telegram:

Dear Aleck,

I find myself in a bit of a jam. If anyone asks you where I was tonight would you mind saying I was with you?

(*signed*) Ross

Actually, it was Connelly who sent the telegram in Ross's name.

Such involuted pranks helped create the atmosphere in which the Algonquin Round Table was conceived; now all that remained was for the twenty-odd habitués to become successful, each according to his or her own natural talents. The speed and seeming felicity with which this second step was accomplished is, in retrospect, the most astonishing characteristic that the Round Tablers shared. The group's average age was not much older than the century itself, and before its members had passed into the next decade, each had achieved his respective niche in contemporary American letters or theater.

The men and women who eventually made up the "Round Table"—or "Vicious Circle," as they preferred calling themselves—came together, as any in-group must, because of mutual interests. To begin with, each possessed, or was possessed by, the spirit of his times, and each, as if touched by a common muse, found natural direction in the urge to record that spirit under the elusive mask of comedy. On the one hand, they embraced the "Roaring Twenties" for the fun-loving hell of it, setting the pace, telling the jokes, pulling the pranks, ignoring the future. As humorist-writer Robert Benchley admitted, "The trouble with me is I can't worry. Damn it, I try to worry, and I can't." On the other hand, they took issue with the general feeling of apathy, the moral and social indifference so characteristic of the period, their humor lashing out at the inadequacies and injustices of the Establishment under which they flourished.

It was not uncommon, if slightly incompatible, for a contingent of Round Tablers to be found gathered at the Puncheon Club or Tony Soma's—two of New York's more popular speakeasies—trading critical jokes on Mayor Walker's corrupt techniques and civic disinterest. Rather than excuse such inconsistencies, they were much more likely to make note of them, usually in a self-deprecating manner, as when Benchley took his first illegal drink, grimaced, and exclaimed, "This place ought to be closed by law!"

In accord with their times, the Algonquin Wits did not take themselves too seriously. Heywood Broun, an ardent social reformer who founded the American Newspaper Guild, once arrived late to dinner at Averell Harriman's and explained, "I was down in the kitchen trying to persuade your butler to strike for higher wages." With Broun and Benchley, as with their comrades in wit, no subject, however solemn or personal, escaped humorous comment. The comic interpretation, whether invoking simple laughter, pathos, or moral disapproval, seemed always to stand as their final statement on whatever issue stirred their fancy.

To discuss such names in the 1960s is rather like reviewing a Who's Who scroll of past American writers and entertainers, with certain outstanding exclusions. But in the early twenties the same names would scarcely have raised an eyebrow. It is important to remember that the Round Tablers sought each other out before they themselves became the sought-after celebrities of Manhattan. Generally speaking, all were young, fun-loving, and ambitious; all took a strong interest in theater, sports, politics, and social problems; and, most noteworthy, all were gregarious, loquacious, articulate.

Their common bond and peculiar genius was, of course, *wit*, although their excellence in conversation, repartee, and bons mots may have caused them to undervalue their contributions to the community of letters.

Alexander Woollcott, called by one critic "the worst writer in America," evidenced this when he said, "I'm potentially the best writer in America, but I never had anything to say." Ring Lardner, perhaps the best-remembered, most respected member of the group, died thinking of himself as a hack writer, successful but second-rate, although Heywood Broun, stating his own regrets, declared on his deathbed that he envied Ring Lardner "because he wrote what he wanted to." Even the widely anthologized Benchley openly regarded himself as a failure. He once remarked, with as much sincerity as irony, "It took me fifteen years to discover that I had no talent for writing, but I couldn't give it up because by that time I was too famous." George Kaufman, who wrote all but one of his shows with a collaborator, referred to himself derisively as "a play doctor." And the others: F.P.A., whose love for the verse form endured as his guiding literary inspiration, considered himself as ultimately a newspaper columnist. Dorothy Parker, as capable a poet as any of her contemporaries, said of herself, wryly, "I was following in the exquisite footsteps of Miss Edna St. Vincent Millay, unhappily in my own horrible sneakers."

Whatever regrets they may have experienced in later life, the Round Tablers of the twenties were far too involved in living to worry about long-range goals. They enjoyed good food and drink, camaraderie, talk, travel, and stud poker. Their daily luncheons were inevitably drawn out well beyond the customary hour. Benchley, who readily admitted his aversion for returning to work after an Algonquin lunch, one day summoned a waiter and handed him a pencil to sharpen, remarking after the tool had been returned, "I may need this some day."

On Saturday nights, Frank Case provided a room upstairs in which the Round Table men, and an occasional woman, gathered under the auspices of the Thanatopsis Literary and Inside Straight Club (F.P.A. founded it, naming it after a similar group of card-playing writers he had formed in Paris while serving on the Army newspaper, *The Stars and Stripes*). They would play poker through the night and often through the remainder of the weekend. Harpo Marx was popularly acknowledged as the most proficient gamester; Woollcott was unanimously voted the worst. As the group grew more prosperous the stakes rose higher and big money became less a subject of awe than an objective reality, lofty but attainable. It was reportedly at a Thanatopsis session that Harold Ross secured a $25,000 stake from millionaire Raoul Fleischmann to start a magazine Ross had dreamed of editing for years and which, at John Peter Toohey's suggestion, he named *The New Yorker*.

Ross, no quipster, proved a striking exception among the Round Table regulars. If his old *Stars and Stripes* buddy, Aleck Woollcott, and their superior officer, Captain Franklin Pierce Adams, were indeed the prototypes of the Algonquin set, then Harold Ross was the original kibitzer, accepted by the others despite the fact that he received more than he contributed. Hard-working—it was said that Ross believed in the twenty-four-hour office-day—straightforward, nonliterary, and never one for verbal calisthentics, Ross nonetheless succeeded in creating and perpetuating a magazine whose idiom, even today, reflects the higher qualities for which the Vicious Circle was noted. His famous "prospectus" for *The New Yorker* owes much to the spirit of the Round Table:

> Its general tenor will be one of gaiety, wit and satire, but it will be more than a jester. It will not be what is commonly called radical or highbrow. It will be what is commonly called sophisticated, in that it will assume a reasonable degree of enlightenment on the part of its readers. It will hate bunk.

With the close of the twenties came the Great Depression and the public lost much of its capacity for laughter. The Algonquin Wits managed to survive on individual grounds, but the Round Table had, for them, lost its lustre, its gaiety. The gilt and sparkle of the Jazz Age had suddenly dissolved, exposing an underlying emptiness. By 1933, Prohibition had come to an end and Wall Street was in the process of rebuilding its crumbled towers. The martini was replacing bathtub gin; even booze had adopted a fresh image, as if its newly acquired respectability qualified it as the businessman's tool instead of his plaything. Lardner was soon to die, followed by Broun's death a few years later. For the rest of the Algonquin group, humor became less a way of life than an artistic commodity which they, as humorists, were obliged to manufacture and sell. The market, while still lucrative, was appreciatively less eager. "Comedy has become like castor oil," said George Kaufman; "people fight it." A disenchanted America had grown sober and restrained; there was, after all, a new war to prepare for, and the economy had all it could manage in the urgent task of regaining its equilibrium.

The Round Table itself, however, has endured. With the *New Yorker* set—led by such later humorists as James Thurber, E. B. White, and Peter Arno—to help span the gap between the Vicious Circle's reign and the present, the famed luncheon spot continues to attract the urbane and sophisticated of each new generation. Go to the Algonquin for lunch on any day of the week, and at today's Round Table (now moved into the Oak Room) you are likely to see such varied personalities as famed trial lawyer Louis Nizer, Court of Appeals Justice Stanley Fuld, British actor Sir Ralph Richardson, Bishop Fulton J. Sheen, *Variety* editor Abel Green, composer Richard Rodgers, cartoonist Harry Hershfield, producer Alexander Cohen, playwright Henry Denker, editor Norman Cousins, publisher and joke-master Bennett Cerf. Dining with them, in a capacity both social and professional, will probably be Ben Bodne, owner of the Algonquin since 1946, and the man most responsible for perpetuating the hotel's tradition as a luncheon stop for Manhattan celebrities.

Ironically, an institution that came to fame because of a rag-tag group of anti-establishmentarians has itself now achieved Establishment status. But when seated at the Round Table, even the dullest Wall Street lawyer finds his wit sharper, his conversation livelier, his repartee saucier. Something of the antic quality of the talk reported in the following pages seems to enter into those who draw up their chairs at the old table.

R.D.

Franklin Pierce Adams

FRANKLIN PIERCE ADAMS (F.P.A.) [1881–1960] *was regarded as the father of the Round Table. His column, "The Conning Tower," spanned a thirty-year period and appeared in three New York newspapers—the* Herald Tribune, *the* World, *and the* Post. *He wrote in the "genteel" tradition, excelling in urbanity, high wit, and erudition. Contributors to "The Conning Tower" included Round Tablers George S. Kaufman, Dorothy Parker, and Alexander Woollcott. Harold Ross based much* New Yorker *humor on "The Conning Tower," liked Adams' emphasis on "humor with a local flavor." Described as "the cigar-smoking, pool-playing little gargoyle with the long neck and the big nose and the bushy mustache," F.P.A. spoke favorably of card games and tennis, derisively of hat-check girls, paper towels, illegible housenumbers, and his wife's salad dressing. Fond of light verse with a satiric bite, he published several books of poetry and short prose sketches (e.g.,* The Book of Diversion *and* Half a Loaf), *and a literary parody in topi-*

cal setting, The Diary of Our Own Samuel Pepys. *He was a regular panelist on the famed "Information, Please" radio show.*

Referring to an occasional Algonquin visitor known for his miserly habits, F.P.A. one day informed the Round Table that the man, newly engaged to be married, had had an accident while buying a ring for his fiancée. "He got his finger crushed between two pushcarts."

One evening at a Thanatopsis session, when Ross was not present, F.P.A. recalled seeing an incredible sight that day—Harold Ross tobogganing.

"For God's sake—Ross tobogganing!" exclaimed Kaufman. "Did he look funny?"

"Well," Adams said, "you know how he looks *not* tobogganing."

Adams, whose philosophical musings generally took expression in the form of backyard aphorisms, once concluded, "Money isn't everything, but lack of money isn't anything."

"The average man is a great deal above the average."

"What this country needs is a good five-cent nickel."

F.P.A. was fond of rewriting advertising slogans for amusement, as with the following razor blade ad: "Ask the man who hones one."

"You may be certain that age is galloping upon you when . . . a feminine voice over the telephone says, 'Do you know who this is?' And you say, 'No,' and hang up the receiver."

The Algonquin has traditionally maintained a policy of issuing personal charge account applications to its regular guests. Filling out one such form, F.P.A. wrote in a space marked Position—"Horizontal."

"In the Countess Salm's letters she said, 'Ludi never was made to work—he hates it.' That is the difference between Ludi and the rest of us, who merely hate it."

"And now Mr. Bernard Shaw says that schoolteachers ought to have babies. Well, he ought to know; he's had schoolteachers."

🖎

"*Il Duce*, believing, as he does, in press censorship, probably will cut the last three words from the headline 'Mussolini Best Man at Marconi's Wedding.'"

🖎

"Our favorite way of wasting time is trying to say something in praise of paper towels."

🖎

"Speaking of screen stars, there's the mosquito."

🖎

"Where the brook of Youth and the river of Age meet is an interesting point. One arrives there when one is too old to rush up to the net and too young to take up the sedentary and ancient game of golf."

🖎

"Our friends accuse us of nepotism. They say our policy is Uncle Sam and Anti-Wilson."

"Ninety-two per cent of the stuff told you in confidence you couldn't get anybody else to listen to."

"As I often have said, I am easily influenced. Compared with me a weather vane is Gibraltar. . . ."

Frank Case in his book *Do Not Disturb*, which was written about the Algonquin, asked F.P.A. to send him a list of his likes and dislikes for publication. F.P.A. responded as follows:
"I like you.
"I dislike parsley, uncrisp bacon, well-done beef.
"You may mention me, and high time, too."

One of the Round Tablers' favorite games was called "I-Can-Give-You-A-Sentence." It involved using a sentence in which a word that sounded like an unrelated phrase was employed. For example, one Christmas season F.P.A. went about wishing all "a meretricious and a happy New Year."

At a Thanatopsis poker session Woollcott remarked in passing, "One thing I'll say for myself, I never struck a woman but once." F.P.A. responded, "And then unfavorably, I'll be bound."

On signing a first-edition copy of his book *Shouts and Murmurs*, Alexander Woollcott sighed and said: "Ah, what is so rare as a Woollcott first edition?"

"A Woollcott second edition," replied F.P.A.

At Thanatopsis poker sessions the Round Table men would generally play through the night (Saturday), and frequently all weekend. At odd intervals one member or another would retire from the game and go home. These persons, according to F.P.A., were suffering from "winner's sleeping sickness," while the remaining players had been stricken with "loser's insomnia," or "Broun's Disease."

F.P.A. once poked good-natured fun at his friend Reginald Birch—the artist, then editor of *Judge*—a man exceptionally small in physical stature: "If you were half a man—and you are."

"The trouble with this country is that there are too many politicians who believe, with a conviction based on experience, that you can fool all of the people all of the time."

"It is a malicious pleasure to think, riding up in the cool Subway, of the motorists driving home through traffic jams; and it is a malicious pleasure to muse, driving home through the fresh air, of the thousands standing up in the hot and sticky Subway."

"Everything, good authority tells us, is lower in price. Even the $5 silk shirts are down to $8.50, reduced from $13.50."

"Every time we tell anybody to cheer up, things might be worse, we run away for fear we might be asked to specify how."

"Our notion of an optimist is a man who, knowing that each year was worse than the preceding, thinks next year will be better. And a pessimist is a man who knows the next year can't be any worse than the last one."

¤

"Watching an aeroplane race, some of the spectators tell us, is more fun than watching a yacht race. The boredom endures less than an hour."

¤

F.P.A. once asked Beatrice Kaufman, "Guess whose birthday it is today?" Beatrice guessed, "Yours?" and F.P.A. admitted, "No, but you're getting warm—it's Shakespeare's."

¤

Heywood Broun, who had taken up oil painting as his chief hobby, once complained to F.P.A., "You have no idea how hard it is to sell a painting."

"If it's so hard," Adams advised, "why don't you try just selling the canvas? I'll give you a note to some tent-makers I know."

¤

Adams belonged to a poker club that numbered among its members a certain actor, Herbert Ransom, whose facial expressions when holding a good hand were so obvious that F.P.A. proposed a new club rule: "Anyone who looks at Ransom's face is cheating."

🎬

F.P.A. once listened painfully but patiently while a friend related a story that threatened never to end. At last the teller drew near his finish and said, "Well, to make a long story short——"

"Too late," said Adams.

🎬

F.P.A., after seeing Helen Hayes' performance in *Caesar and Cleopatra*, remarked that the young actress seemed to be suffering from "fallen archness."

🎬

While in France serving on the *Stars and Stripes*, Captain F. P. Adams inscribed a book to Medical Sergeant Aleck Woollcott—then, as later, an exceedingly hefty man. The inscription recalled crowded conditions in Paris, when, rank being disregarded, officers and men were sometimes forced to bunk together:

> One night I slept on a
> Terribly full cot,
> My partner being
> Alexander Woollcott.

On the birth of a baby boy to actress Myra Hampton, the members of the Thanatopsis Literary and Inside Straight Club—who all thought highly of her—chipped in and gave the young actress a share of United States Steel, worth over $200, in the infant's name. A short time later Wall Street crashed, and F.P.A. remarked at the club's next meeting, "I hear Myra's kid has been clipped by the market."

F.P.A. once escorted George and Beatrice Kaufman to a cocktail party where Beatrice, sitting down on a cane-bottom chair, suddenly broke through the seat. Held captive by the frame, her derrière drooping to the floor, Beatrice looked to the men for help. Adams secured her humiliation by remarking, 'I've told you a hundred times, Beatrice, that's not funny!"

At the close of the football season one year F.P.A. decided that as long as so many persons were choosing All-American teams, he might as well pick one himself. Following were his nominations: "Cedars of Lebanon; Diet of Rice; Crossing of Delaware; Bells of St. Mary's; Dissolution of Union; Quality of Mercer; Heart of Maryland; District of Columbia; Pillars of Temple; Grist of

Mills; and Destruction of Carthage."

Substitutes included: "Hard, Knox; Dead, Center; Gimme, De Pauw."

🖋

Adams once discussed the etiquette involved in a young man's seeing a young woman home from a date. He stressed that this was not always a clear-cut situation, and that the varying desires of the two players often made it difficult for them to know what to say. He explained this as follows:

Four things are possible:

1. He wants to come in and she wants him to.

2. He wants to come in and she doesn't want him to.

3. He doesn't want to come in and she wants him to.

4. He doesn't want to come in and she doesn't want him to.

Well——

1

"You don't think I'm going home, do you?"
"I should say not."

2

"I'm coming in."
"Oh, no, you're not."

3

"Well, good night."

"Aren't you coming in to say good night to me?"

"No, I can't."

"Why not?"

"I've got to get up early tomorrow."

"Oh, just for a few minutes."

"No, I can't."

"Oh, please. Just a few minutes."

"No, I've got to go to bed. If I don't get my eight hours I'm no good the next day."

"Oh, what's five minutes?"

"It'll be more than that."

"No, I'll send you away in five minutes."

"Will you, honest?"

"Yes, my dear."

"All right."

4

"Good night."

"Night."

Adams had short patience with boring conversationalists and seldom could bring himself to listen to them, even as a polite gesture. One evening at the Players, spotting a well-known bore headed in his direction, F.P.A. met his adversary, took his hand, and said, "How are you that's fine," then went his way, leaving the man alone and confused in the center of the room.

One of the members of a poker group to which F.P.A. belonged was an especially long-winded storyteller much of whose material centered around the famous baseball pitcher Christy Mathewson, his personal friend. One night when the man was absent, the news came in that Mathewson had died. One of the players observed, "This will cut down his conversational stock fifty per cent."

"A drop in the bucket," Adams cracked.

F.P.A. dedicated his book *Overset* to New York *World* editor Herbert Bayard Swope. The dedication page read:

To
HERBERT BAYARD SWOPE
without whose friendly
aid and counsel every
line in this book was
written

At a Players Club gathering one of the members held the floor in denunciation of a generally unpopular fellow member, ending his comments with the relatively soft statement, "He's his own worst enemy." "Not while I'm around," said F.P.A.

On the occasion of a well-publicized theater fire in the Basque country of Spain (in which a number of patrons were crushed and killed trying to escape through the building's one door), F.P.A. philosophized, "Don't put all your Basques in one exit."

"When politicians appeal to all intelligent voters, they mean everyone who is going to vote for them."

When Woollcott moved to his East River address—later to be christened "Wit's End" by Dorothy Parker—he sent out invitations to his friends to give him a linen-china-and-silver "shower." F.P.A. obligingly sent him a handkerchief, a moustache cup, and a dime.

Though Dorothy Parker's appellation for Woollcott's apartment on the East River—"Wit's End"—proved more lasting, F.P.A. suggested one that many favored: "Old Manse River."

" 'Big wars,' says the *Herald Tribune,* in our nomination for the year's Half-Truth Prize, 'are very costly to the losers.' "

" 'Does civilization pay?' asks the Reverend Dr. Arthur Wakefield Slater. Yes, but only about ten cents on the dollar."

"About censorship we feel the way either Mr. Moran or Mr. Mack feels about piccolo playing. 'Even if it's good,' drawls the drawling one, 'I won't like it.' "

One night Woollcott showed up at a Thanatopsis game wearing a $200 bearskin coat which he had bought before the war, and which, he boasted, could be sold any day for as much as he had paid for it. F.P.A. glanced over at the always unkempt Heywood Broun and said, "You couldn't get that much for your entire wardrobe, Heywood . . . unless it was from a costumer."

On one October evening, while vacationing in Sag Harbor with the Frank Cases (Algonquin owners), F.P.A. politely watched from the dock while a number of the other guests engaged in chilly water-sports. Back in the house, after what seemed to him too much time had elapsed between entertainment and refreshments, F.P.A. said, "What do you have to do to get a drink around here—turn up embalmed in a glacier, like the Lost Bridegroom?"

At a Thanatopsis session, F.P.A., who professed to be a garden lover, reported that his peonies required special attention. One of the members asked, "How about your dahlias?"

"They're thriving," F.P.A. answered. "It proves that if you take care of your peonies, the dahlias will look after themselves."

"Nothing is more responsible for the good old days than a bad memory."

Robert Benchley

ROBERT BENCHLEY [1889–1945] *was a drama critic for twenty years, first with the old* Life *magazine, then with* The New Yorker. *As a well-known humorist-writer, he contributed countless short pieces, gently sardonic in tone, to popular magazines. Many of these were collected in book form, under such titles as* Of All Things, My Ten Years in a Quandary, Chips Off the Old Benchley. *He later wrote, directed, and acted in humorous film shorts. He was once described as "a sly wag with an inexact mustache, a burbling laugh and one of the world's warmest wits." His writings were said to be "only one of the outward and visible evidences of the inner grace, the divine essence," which led one commentator to write, "Benchley was humor." As an American wit, Benchley made a clear break from the "crackerbox philosopher" tradition, choosing a style both sophisticated and literate. He edited the* Harvard Lampoon *while an undergraduate, later retaining his interest in satire, parody, and verbal understatement, as in "The Treasurer's Re-*

port." A strong "nonsense element" dominates much of his written and spoken humor.

Better than anyone else, Benchley recognized his own irresponsibility in matters of finance. He once applied for a loan at his local bank and, to his shock, was granted the money with no questions asked. The next day he reportedly withdrew all his savings from the bank, explaining, "I don't trust a bank that would lend money to such a poor risk."

Benchley lived at the Algonquin for a period, later moving across the street to another hotel. He explained to owner Frank Case that too many friends had the habit of milling around the Algonquin lobby and coming up to visit him. Case suggested that Benchley tell the desk clerks not to let anyone up until he had given them a telephone okay. "Yes," said Benchley, "but that won't keep *me* from coming down."

Benchley once appended a note to his endorsement on the back of a bank check: "Having a wonderful time, wish you were here. Robert Rabbit Benchley."

ON MIRRORS: "Things are depressing enough as they are, without my going out of my way to make myself miserable."

"A man gets on a train with his little boy, and gives the conductor only one ticket. 'How old's your kid?' the conductor says, and the father says he's four years old. 'He looks at least twelve to me,' says the conductor, and the father says, 'Can I help it if he worries?' "

"There are various forms of a [certain] disease, the victim of which is unable to say 'No.' Some of these forms are more serious than others, and often lead to electrocution or marriage."

"With the increase in crime during the past decade has come a corresponding increase in crime prevention. Or perhaps it is vice versa."

Influenced by an irrepressible New England conscience regarding sex, Benchley expressed outward disapproval of sensationalism as a marketable commodity in the theater. Discussing the play *Ception Shoals*, starring Nazimova, Benchley found the production "too obstetric for my simple soul," and referred to its starring lady as the play's "leading spermatozoa."

◆

In 1930, Benchley commented on his reputation as a bad businessman, a weakness he readily admitted: "Of course, if I wanted to, I might point out that out of a possible $5,000 which I have made since I left school I have had $3,000 worth of good food (all of which has gone into making bone and muscle and some nice fat), $1,500 worth of theater tickets, and $500 worth of candy; whereas many of my business friends have simply had $5,000 worth of whatever that stock was which got so yellow along about last November."

◆

Benchley spent a short, highly unsuccessful apprenticeship in the advertising department of Curtis Publishing Company, about which he recalled: "When I left Curtis (I was given plenty of time to get my hat and coat) I was advised not to stick to advertising. They said I was too tall, or something. I forget just what the reason was they gave."

◆

On a summer vacation trip Benchley arrived in Venice and immediately wired a friend: "STREETS FLOODED. PLEASE ADVISE."

Benchley once wrote a magazine article called "I Like to Loaf." When the editor received the piece a full two weeks late, it included a note which read: "I was loafing."

After lunching with a friend one afternoon at a Manhattan restaurant, Benchley insisted on paying the check but the friend objected with equal determination. Beckoning to the waiter, Benchley said, "Don't pay any attention to my nephew. He spent his allowance last night at the roller rink."

"The advantage of keeping family accounts is clear. If you do not keep them, you are uneasily aware of the fact that you are spending more than you are earning. If you do keep them, you *know* it."

"Tell us your phobias and we will tell you what you are afraid of."

"A dog teaches a boy fidelity, perseverance, and to turn around three times before lying down."

🏴

Discussing a Broadway show: "It was one of those plays in which all the actors unfortunately enunciated very clearly."

🏴

ON SLEEP: "If we can develop some way in which a man can *doze* (in public) and still keep from making a monkey of himself, we have removed one of the big obstacles to human happiness in modern civilization."

🏴

"There is a certain type of citizen (a great many times, I am sorry to have to say, one of the fair sex) whose lack of civic pride shows itself in divers forms, but it is in the devastation of a Sunday newspaper that it reaches full bloom. Show me a Sunday paper which has been left in a condition fit only for kite flying, and I will show you an antisocial and dangerous character who has left it that way."

🏴

"In Milwaukee last month a man died laughing over one of his own jokes. That's what makes it so tough for us outsiders. We have to fight home competition."

"You have no idea how many problems an author has to face during those feverish days when he is building a novel, and you have no idea how he solves them. Neither has he."

Coming out of a midtown restaurant, Benchley spotted a uniformed man at the door. "Would you get us a taxi, please," he asked the man. "I'm sorry," the man said coldly, "I happen to be a rear admiral in the United States Navy." "All right, then," said Benchley, "get us a battleship."

Six days after Lindbergh's historic flight to LeBourget, Benchley sent a telegram to his friend Charles Brackett in Paris: "ANY TIDINGS OF LINDBERGH? LEFT HERE WEEK AGO. AM WORRIED."

Benchley and Dorothy Parker shared a tiny $30-a-month office for a time in the Metropolitan Opera House studios. As Benchley described it, "One cubic foot less of space and it would have constituted adultery."

"It took me fifteen years to discover that I had no talent for writing, but I couldn't give it up because by that time I was too famous."

On the death of a Hollywood movie queen whose sensational love-life had been highly publicized, Benchley suggested an epitaph: "She sleeps alone at last."

Once, when asked whether he knew the six-foot-seven playwright Robert Sherwood, Benchley climbed onto a chair and extended his hand to just below the ceiling: "Why, I've known Bob Sherwood since he was *this* high."

At one point during the twenties most of the Round Tablers were finding personal success for the first time. "It must be a boom," observed Georges, the Algonquin's headwaiter; "they order ice cream on top of everything." Benchley added calmly, "And then they grab their lollipops and pitter-patter over to their psychiatrists."

In the hospital just before he died, Benchley occupied himself in reading a book of philosophical essays called *The Practical Cogitator, or, The Thinker's Anthology* The last essay he read, by James Harvey Robinson, was titled "Am I Thinking?" A marginal notation beside the title read: "No. (And supposing you were?)"

Abie's Irish Rose, one of the most spectacular smash-hits in Broadway history, was panned by most serious theater critics. Benchley was adamant in his opinion of it: *"The Rotters* [also a notoriously poor play] is no longer the worst play in town! *Abie's Irish Rose* has just opened." His subsequent comments about the show during its record run from June of 1922 to November of 1927 included these:

"People laugh at this every night, which explains why democracy can never be a success."

"In another two or three years, we'll have this play driven out of town."

"Where do people come from who keep this going? You don't see them out in the daytime."

"We were only fooling all the time. It's a great show." Then, much later:

"We might as well say it now as later. We don't like this play."

Recalling his college days, Benchley once made up a list of lessons learned during his four-year stint. Following are a few examples of knowledge he noted as gained during his freshman year:

1. Charlemagne either died or was born or did something with the Holy Roman Empire in 800.

2. By placing one paper bag inside another paper bag you can carry home a milkshake in it.

3. There is a double "l" in the middle of "parallel."

4. Powder rubbed on the chin will take the place of a shave if the room isn't very light.

5. French nouns ending in "aison" are feminine.

6. Almost everything you need to know about a subject is in the encyclopedia.

Five days before sailing on a trip to Europe, Benchley decided to take his mother along—she was then 79—so that she might visit her niece and nephew-in-law in Paris. Benchley cabled the couple ahead of time: "MOTHER WANTS TO KNOW WHETHER TO BRING HER BICYCLE."

A scene in one of his numerous movie shorts required Benchley to be strung up in a mess of telephone wires above a city street. While waiting for the final camera, he called to his wife, Gertrude, who was on location: "Remember how good in Latin I was in school?"

"I do," she replied.

"Well, look where it got me."

"It takes no great perspicacity to detect and to complain of the standardization in American life. So many foreign and domestic commentators have pointed this feature out in exactly the same terms that the comment has become standardized and could be turned out by the thousands on little greeting cards, all from the same typeform: 'American life has become too standardized.' "

In a piece called "Literary Lost and Found Department" Benchley parodied the literary queries in the *New York Times Book Review*. Here is one of his entries:

K.L.F.—Who wrote the following and what does it mean?

"Oh, de golden wedding,
Oh, de golden wedding,
Oh, de golden wedding,
De golden, golden wedding!"

A friend once told Benchley that a particular drink he was drinking was slow poison, to which Benchley replied, "So who's in a hurry?"

🏴

One young lady who occasionally visited the Round Table was known to have made several half-hearted attempts at suicide. After one of her recent efforts Benchley cautioned her: "You want to go easy on this suicide stuff. First thing you know, you'll ruin your health."

🏴

Arriving home with a group of friends one rainy evening, Benchley suggested (though some have attributed the remark to Aleck Woollcott), "Let's get out of these wet clothes and into a dry martini."

🏴

"I haven't been abroad in so long that I almost speak English without an accent."

🏴

"In America there are two classes of travel—first class and with children."

"The biggest obstacle to professional writing today is the necessity for changing a typewriter ribbon."

"My college education was no haphazard affair. My courses were all selected with a very definite aim in view, with a serious purpose in mind—no classes before eleven in the morning or after two-thirty in the afternoon, and nothing on Saturday at all—on that rock was my education built."

Commenting on the fact that one measure suggested to aid in reducing automobile accidents was the prohibition of gasoline sales to drunk drivers, Benchley made a list of infallible symptoms of intoxication in drivers—for the benefit of gas-station attendants. Following are some of the key symptoms:

When the driver is sitting with his back against the instrument panel and his feet on the driver's seat.

When the people in the back seat are crouched down on the floor with their arms over their heads.

When the driver points to the gas-tank and says, "A pound of liver, please."

If the driver insists that the gas-station man take the

driver's seat while he (the driver) fills the tank, first exchanging hats.

When the driver goes into the rest-room and doesn't come out.

When the driver is alone and stark naked.

When there is no driver at all.

"Merely as an observer of natural phenomena, I am fascinated by my own personal appearance. This doesn't mean that I am *pleased* with it, mind you, or that I can even tolerate it. I simply have a morbid interest in it."

In Hollywood on a warm, bright day Benchley was found by a friend sitting under a sun-lamp in his room. When the friend asked why he didn't go outside to get his sun, Benchley exclaimed, "And get hit by a meteor?"

While a student at Harvard, Benchley came across a final exam question that read: "Discuss the arbitration of the international fisheries problem in respect to hatcheries protocol and dragnet and trawl procedure as it affects (a) the point of view of the United States, and (b) the point of view of Great Britain."

Benchley answered with a mixture of directness and evasion: "I know nothing about the point of view of Great Britain in the arbitration of the international fisheries problem, and nothing about the point of view of the United States. Therefore I shall discuss the question from the point of view of the fish."

"I do most of my work sitting down. That's where I shine."

"There are several ways in which to apportion the family income, all of them unsatisfactory."

"Anyone can do any amount of work, provided it isn't the work he is supposed to be doing."

Leaving Hollywood's Garden of Allah Hotel to return to New York, Benchley handed out final tips to everyone who had waited on him, after which he was approached by a doorman he hadn't seen during his entire stay. "Aren't you going to remember me?" the doorman asked, holding out his hand. "Why, of course," Benchley answered, "I'll write you every day."

🏴

After graduating from Harvard, Benchley took a job for a time organizing employee clambakes for a Boston paper company. Reminiscing about this brief occupation, Benchley confessed, "I've never looked a clam in the face since."

🏴

"A great many people have come up to me and asked how I manage to get so much work done and still keep looking so dissipated. My answer is, 'Don't you wish you knew?' and a pretty good answer it is, too, when you consider that nine times out of ten I didn't hear the original question."

🏴

In his book *The Time of Laughter* Corey Ford relates a story that took place when Benchley was serving as an editor on the old *Life*. During that period, Ford himself was contributing articles to *Life*, and by coincidence another writer, named Torrey Ford, was doing the same. Corey asked Benchley's advice on how to avoid confusion of identities, and Benchley suggested, "You could print your stuff in a different color ink, but that might run into expense. Maybe the best idea would be to let Torrey handle the articles, and you handle the checks."

Benchley was known for carrying on a constant war with machines and inanimate objects, always coming out the loser. Once he wrote: "The hundred and one little bits of wood and metal that go to make up the impedimenta of our daily life . . . each and every one are bent on my humiliation and working together, as on one great team, to bedevil and confuse me and to get me into a neurasthenics' home before I am sixty. I can't fight these boys. They've got me licked."

Robert Sherwood told a story about Benchley which took place when both they and Dorothy Parker were working for *Vanity Fair*. The magazine followed a policy—which the three young editors found undignified and rather childish—requiring tardy employees to explain the reason for their lateness on cards. One morning Benchley arrived late; he promptly filled out both sides of a card, explaining that he had been "detained by rounding up a herd of elephants that had escaped from the Hippodrome," which resulted in his being eleven minutes late getting to work.

Benchley loved parties and invariably managed to be the last guest to leave. He was somewhat piqued by the way certain people could arise with no trouble, say something like "I guess it's time to be going," and leave. Once he commented, "I can't seem to bring myself to say, 'Well I guess I'll be toddling along . . .' It isn't that I can't toddle. It's that I can't guess I'll toddle."

Heywood Broun

HEYWOOD BROUN [1888—1939], *as columnist for several New York papers, was as an ardent crusader for the underdog. He championed many causes through his "It Seems to Me" column, which ran for a twenty-year period. In it, he attacked such things as capital punishment, labor spies, Mayor Rolph's approval of San Jose lynchings. He pleaded for Sacco and Vanzetti, the Scottsboro boys, and the Gastonia strikers, and, with Dorothy Parker, headed the Joint Anti-Fascist Refugee Committee to raise funds for Spanish Republicans. His article "A Union for Reporters" roused that formerly indifferent group into forming the American Newspaper Guild, of which he became president (1933). A man of huge physical proportions and a strikingly unkempt appearance, he was once described as "a peculiarly lovable mass of contradictions . . . soft-hearted, steel-minded, brave and terrified, considerate and tough, gregarious and solitary." Possessed of a clever wit, Broun was generally reflective and philosophical but when dealing with social injustice he was capable of harshness. He began his newspaper career as drama critic for the New York World.*

At a newsmen's banquet President Harding appeared as guest speaker and delivered what struck Broun as the epitome of cliché-ridden, *ghost-written* addresses. After a brief moment of respectful applause, Broun rose from his chair and cried, "Author! Author!"

Appearing bleary-eyed and sleepless at a Chicago convention, Broun remarked: "I came out in a lower from New York and couldn't sleep a wink: a dwarf in the upper above me kept chasing up and down all night."

As a play reviewer Broun was usually gentle, but one actor's performance so displeased him that he was moved to classify the young man, Geoffrey Steyne, as the worst actor on the American stage. Steyne sued, but the case was dismissed. The next time Broun reviewed a play in which Steyne appeared, he made no mention of the actor until the last sentence, which read, "Mr. Steyne's performance was not up to its usual standard."

In 1935, Broun made this statement: "Nobody need worry any more that Washington is going left. Indeed, nobody need worry that the Washington of today is going anywhere."

Broun, known for his always unkempt appearance, devoted an article to the topic "Best-Dressed Women of the World." In it he commented on his own experience in such contests: "While I was running for Best-Dressed Senior in the graduating class of Horace Mann High School I often spent as much as three or four minutes in the morning deciding which pants I ought to wear. They grey or the blue. The blue or the grey. I generally decided to take the ones which possessed the closest approach to a crease."

On a voyage across the Pacific, Broun and his fellow passengers one day decided to provide themselves with an evening of entertainment. Heywood was asked to box three rounds with a man whose stature closely matched his own 240-pound frame. Before accepting the offer, Heywood engaged the other fellow in a chat, presumably to discover what he was up against. In the course of their talk, the man said to Heywood, "I'm going to ask you a question which I have wanted to ask someone ever since I got on this ship. What is this 'demitasse' they have on the bill of fare?" Heywood later sought out the chairman of the entertainment committee and announced, "I've changed my mind about boxing with that chap. Any man who doesn't know what a 'demitasse' is *must* be a tough guy."

Broun the columnist was accustomed to hearing such comments at social gatherings as "I always read your column, but I don't always agree with it." Once, spotting columnist General Hugh S. Johnson across the room, Heywood approached him and said: "General, I always agree with your column, but I never read it."

On his first meeting with Ruth Hale, whom he later married, Broun took the young lady for a stroll in Central Park, where she became intrigued with a squirrel which had come begging for food. After listening to Miss Hale's repeated regrets that she had no peanuts to give the squirrel, Broun remarked, "I can't help you except to give him a nickel so he can go and buy his own."

One February, Broun quoted this statement in his "It Seems to Me" column: "York, Pa.—With the temperature at 10 degrees below zero, the first robin of the year was seen in York yesterday. It was found dead on Penn Common."

Discussing boorishness in public places, especially in theaters where "ermined" and "sabled" ladies make concentration somewhat difficult, Broun remarked, "I want some day to see a Broadway opening without benefit of footnotes. I'd rather not be told by the lady just ahead that a line is 'delicious' or 'so quaint.' I'd rather be surprised."

"There is no lantern by which the *crank* can be distinguished from the *reformer* when the night is dark. Just as every conviction begins as a whim so does every emancipator serve his apprenticeship as a crank. A fanatic is a great leader who is just entering the room."

"Public opinion in this country runs like a shower bath. We have no temperatures between hot and cold."

During the run of a Broadway show in which Tallulah Bankhead was starring, Broun whispered to the actress, "Don't look now, Tallulah, but your show's slipping."

Broun once referred to Alexander Woollcott as "the smartest of Alecs."

"A liberal is a man who leaves the room when the fight starts."

"She leads away from aces and neglects to keep jump bids alive. But she is still my mother."

"Frantic arguments go on and charts and graphs are presented to show that things are better, much worse or just the same. It all depends upon the chartmaker, where the design appears, and whether you have the blame thing right side up."

Broun, who was totally captivated by the Marx Brothers, went to see their shows—each one—as many times as possible (he saw *Cocoanuts* twenty-one times). Concerning this particular passion, he remarked: "Very likely my epitaph will read, 'Here lies Heywood Broun (Who?), killed by getting in the way of some scene shifters at a Marx Brothers show.'"

One "I-Can-Give-You-A-Sentence" story Broun was fond of telling involved an overgrown papoose whom the chief expelled from the tribe, saying, "You big! Quit us." "That," he would explain, "is the origin of 'ubiquitous.'"

"Any port in a storm," Broun once remarked on taking a drink of "a certain inferior liquor."

Broun said of one fence-straddling radio commentator, "His mind is so open that the wind whistles through it."

Heywood's mother, who was as conservative as he was liberal, once said to him (as Broun reported it): "The trouble with you, Heywood, is that you have never been an employer."

Discussing the difference between his mother's political views and his own left-wing tendencies, Broun remarked, "When the revolution comes it's going to be a tough problem what to do with her. We will either have to shoot her or make her a commissar. In the meantime we still dine together."

Referring to the popularity of sensational, "sexy" books, which he felt was unwarranted, Broun made this observation: "Obscenity is such a tiny kingdom that a single tour covers it completely."

Arriving late at a Thanksgiving weekend party given by the Averell Harrimans, Broun (by then a union leader) alibied: "I was down in the kitchen trying to persuade your butler to strike for higher wages."

At the time when the Sacco-Vanzetti appeal from their death sentences was rejected, Heywood referred to Harvard University, some of whose officials had opposed his stand on the case, as "Hangman's House."

"The only real argument for Marriage is that it remains the best method for getting acquainted."

In 1933, Broun commented on the state of the theater in New York: "Nothing could have been sicker than the New York stage just one year ago. Practically all the playhouses had gone back to the Indians or the savings banks. Whenever anybody saw a light in any of the theaters he immediately called the police and informed them that mothball burglars were on the rampage once again."

"The ability to make love frivolously is the chief characteristic which distinguishes human beings from the beasts."

"I have known people to stop and buy an apple on the corner and then walk away as if they had solved the unemployment problem."

"Many people [in the city] buy a house just to get the trees which are thrown in with the deal. I've got three and a large part of the overhang from a tree next door. This trespasser, from a strictly material standpoint, is a finer tree than any which I possess, but I prefer my own horse chestnut just the same. It's a one-man tree and would never think of dividing its loyalty between two houses."

"The trouble with me is that I inherited an insufficient amount of vengeful feeling. Kings, princes, dukes, and even local squires rode their horses so that they stepped upon the toes of my ancestors, who did nothing about it except to apologize. I would then have joined most eagerly in pulling down the Bastille, but if anybody had caught me at it and given me a sharp look I'm afraid I would have put it back again."

"Some of my best friends are newspaper photographers. . . . And yet I feel that when one or two are gathered together for professional reasons you have a nuisance, and that a dozen or more constitute a plague."

"I'd rather be right than Roosevelt."

Discussing popular images of newspapermen, Broun said, "There are exceptions, but when a play includes 'Jim Swift—Reporter of the *Times-Telegram*' you can be pretty sure that presently there will appear a character compounded out of Iago and the protagonist in *Ten Nights in a Barroom.*"

"I remember once a dramatist was hailed as a great realist because the reporter in his play was shown with a copy of *The American Mercury* in one pocket and a quart of whiskey in the other."

Feeling guilty about his occasional hobby of fishing, Broun once wrote, "It is not fair that I should thwart and crush great eagerness for existence for the sake of the extremely mild diversion which I get from fishing. They told me that the fish cared very little and that they were cold-blooded and felt no pain. But they were not fish who told me."

"Any reasonable system of taxation should be based on the slogan of 'Soak the rich.'"

"You might not mind so much if your sister married one of them, and two or three asked in after dinner would not for a certainty spoil the party, but taken as a group the drama critics of New York are so much suet pudding."

"I was a child prodigy myself. That is, at the age of five I already required twelve-year-old pants."

One morning, finding a self-analysis questionnaire on his desk, Broun included some of the questions with his answers in that day's column:

"*What is my occupation?* Newspaperman.

"*Am I making a success of it?* There seems to be a decided difference of opinion.

"*What is my character and reputation?* Unreliable and charming.

"*What do other men think of me?* Unreliable.

"*What do I think of myself?* Charming.

"*Am I cleanly?* Very much so in the summer.

"*Punctual?* No.

"*Courteous?* To a fault.

"*Have I any definite object in life?* Yes. I want to be a writer.

"*Am I on my way?* Not precipitately."

After a minor operation, Heywood composed the following lyric for his surgeon:

> There was a young man with a hernia
> Who said to his surgeon, "Gol-dernya,
> When carving my middle
> Be sure you don't fiddle
> With matters that do not concernya."

In 1935, following talk of the end of the Depression, Broun offered President Roosevelt a new slogan: "Pinch yourself and see if you're prosperous."

Heywood obviously was not speaking for himself or his Round Table cronies when he stated: "Repartee is what you wish you'd said."

"Hell is paved with great granite blocks hewn from the hearts of those who said, 'I can do no other.' "

ON HUMOR:

"Humor is the coward's livery, and there is great wisdom in the popular challenge, 'Laugh that off.' "

"Humor is grit in the evolutionary process. 'Does it matter?' is the underlying mood in almost every expression of humor. And of course it does matter."

George S. Kaufman

GEORGE S. KAUFMAN [1889–1961], *called the "gloomy dean of American humor," associated in the authorship of more than forty plays and musical comedies. He won two Pulitzer Prizes, for* Of Thee I Sing, *written with* Morrie Ryskind, *and* You Can't Take It With You, *with* Moss Hart. *Kaufman preferred to work with a collaborator, writing only one successful play on his own,* The Butter and Egg Man. *As playwright, producer, and director, he literally reigned on Broadway for more than twenty years, while appearing regularly on radio ("Information, Please") and television ("This Is Show Business"). His comedies were farcical, fast-moving, gagfilled, and usually mocking in tone. His verbal wit could be sharp and cutting and often cynical. His adroitness with language made him a master at punning. Shy, retiring and outwardly nervous, Kaufman remained a hardworking artist and businessman, holding onto his post as* New York Times *drama critic long after he had succeeded with several Broadway shows.*

During the influenza epidemic of 1918, just after his first play had opened in New York, Kaufman reportedly went around advising people to "avoid crowds—see *Someone in the House.*"

As a young theater critic and aspiring playwright, Kaufman was assigned to cover a new Broadway comedy. In his review he wrote: "There was laughter in the back of the theater, leading to the belief that somebody was telling jokes back there."

After the flop of his first play, *Someone in the House,* Kaufman remarked, "there wasn't."

Kaufman and Charlie Chaplin once got into a discussion about personal health. At one point Chaplin announced with pride that his blood pressure was "down to 108."

"Common or preferred?" Kaufman inquired.

One dark, stormy night Kaufman joined Frank Sullivan and Edna Ferber for dinner at a Manhattan restaurant. Over the course of the evening their conversation grew so morbid that G.S.K. suddenly informed the others that he wanted to commit suicide. "How, George?" asked Miss Ferber, somewhat concerned.

"With kindness," Kaufman answered.

🚩

"Massey won't be satisfied until he's assassinated," Kaufman remarked about actor Raymond Massey's heralded performance in *Abe Lincoln in Illinois*.

🚩

Kaufman once visited the office of Jed Harris, the theater producer, and was received by the unpredictable tycoon stark naked. Accustomed to Harris' flights of pretentious fancy, Kaufman addressed him calmly: "Mr. Harris, your fly is open."

🚩

Kaufman collaborated with Morrie Ryskind and George and Ira Gershwin on the musical *Strike Up the Band*. During the show's Philadelphia tryout, which was a financial failure, someone approached Kaufman in his hotel lobby and asked, "Mr. Gershwin, why is this show so bad? I loved your music."

"The show is bad because George Kaufman wrote the book," G.S.K. replied.

Conducting a survey for a question-and-answer book he was editing, George Oppenheimer once quizzed Kaufman on geography—a subject that throughly bored G.S.K. One of the questions read: "What is the longest river in South America?"

After a moment of feigned deliberation, Kaufman queried, "Are you sure it's in South America?"

🪲

While entertaining musician-wit Oscar Levant at his new Bucks County home, George Kaufman offered his friend an engaging business proposition (based on Levant's reputation as a noxious influence): "We'll both walk through the main thoroughfares of Bucks County and I'll have blueprints in my hand and this will lead people to think that you are going to build and settle down here. The local inhabitants will become panic-stricken and real estate will go down. Then we'll buy, you won't build, and we'll clean up."

🪲

During a late-hour Thanatopsis game, G.S.K. drew a poor poker hand, studied it in disgust, and announced, "I have been traydeuced."

🪲

At a Round Table gathering, the subject of Aleck Woollcott's inevitable failure to marry came under discussion, with Kaufman offering an explanation: "A man sometimes fails to marry because, literally, any one of the women he might want to marry cannot reach him." When someone complained that G.S.K.'s explanation was a trifle obscure, and asked for further clarification, Kaufman said, "It's quite simple. Have you ever taken a good look at our friend's paunch?"

Of the play *Skylark*, which starred Gertrude Lawrence, G.S.K. declared, "It was a bad play saved by a bad performance."

On being asked to describe Alexander Woollcott in one word, G.S.K. concentrated for a moment, then answered, "Improbable."

"How many persons," the playwright once said, "even among your best friends, really hope for your success on an opening night? A failure is somehow so much more satisfying all around."

Kaufman once cracked: "Satire is something that closes on Saturday night."

During the 30's, for a period of three to four years, G.S.K. listened to Marc Connelly tell of his alleged progress on a new play. At one point during that period Simon and Schuster (publishers) discovered and published a previously unknown Charles Dickens manuscript entitled *Life of Our Lord*. Kaufman observed, "Charles Dickens, dead, writes more than Marc Connelly alive."

One evening Raoul Fleischmann remarked during a Thanatopsis game that he was fourteen before he realized that he was a Jew. "That's nothing," said Kaufman. "I was sixteen before I knew I was a boy."

Kaufman once voiced a possible solution to New York City's traffic problem: "Have all the traffic lights on the streets turn red—and keep them that way."

Discussing his first employer, a comptroller for whom he worked as a stenographer, Kaufman remarked, "His title worried me. Finally I figured out that it means a man who begins dictating letters at fifteen minutes to six."

Kaufman was seldom open to outside suggestions concerning his work, especially from persons he didn't know. One self-appointed critic, on being snubbed by G.S.K., remarked, "Perhaps you don't realize who I am?"

"That's only part of it," said Kaufman.

On the Lucy Stone League—which held, among other things, that women were entitled to keep their individual identities in marriage—G.S.K. commented: "A Lucy Stone gathers no boss."

Playing "I-Can-Give-You-A-Sentence," G.S.K. said to Frank Case, "I know a farmer who has two daughters, Lizzie and Tillie. Lizzie is all right, but you have no idea how punctilious."

Kaufman once stated that had it not been for a certain postcard that was lost in the mails—one introducing him as an actor instead of a writer—he might have become a celebrated star. "And today," he added, "Eugene O'Neill would still be America's foremost playwright."

In an article for *The New York Times Magazine,* Kaufman wrote: "Having listened for many years to the dramatic opinions of all kinds of persons, I would like to suggest a basic change in the manner of printing the phone directory, so that this generally secondary profession may receive recognition. 'Baldwin, Walter J.,' I would have it say, 'furs and dramatic critic.' 'Stuffnagel, Rufus W., garbage collector and dramatic critic.' And so on."

Speaking of Boston as a try-out city for potential Broadway plays, Kaufman said: "In Boston the test of a play is simple. If the play is bad the pigeons snarl at you as you walk across the Common."

"When I was born I owed twelve dollars."

Kaufman told this story about his young daughter. She went to see *Pride and Prejudice* while it was playing across the street from *First Lady,* a comedy he had co-authored. "Daddy," she told him later, "when I left the theater I looked across the street and saw only three people leaving your theater. The attendance must have fallen off terribly."

Kaufman explained that *First Lady* was a longer play, so that it ended fifteen minutes later than *Pride and Prejudice*.

"So," the girl returned, "they were walking out on you, eh?"

On the movie set of *Stage Door*, which Kaufman referred to as "Screen Door," the playwright and his co-author, Edna Ferber, became exasperated while trying to cast a woman pianist who could act, or vice versa. At one point Kaufman remarked, "It begins to appear, my dear Edna, that we are trying to find a hen's tooth that can recite 'Gunga Din' with feeling."

Kaufman wrote the comedy *Cocoanuts* (in collaboration with Morrie Ryskind and Irving Berlin) for his friends the Marx Brothers. Concerning this experience, Kaufman said, "*Cocoanuts* introduced me to the Marx Brothers. *Cocoanuts* was a comedy, the Marx Brothers are comics, meeting them was a tragedy."

While rehearsing *Cocoanuts*, Kaufman and the Marx Brothers fell into an argument over a piece of stage business. Groucho, in an attempt to justify his stand, remarked, "Well, they laughed at Fulton and his steamboat."

"Not at matinees," replied Kaufman.

Eleanor Roosevelt told of the time when Kaufman, after dining at the White House, said to her, "You have a good location, good food, and I'm sure the place should be a great success when it's noised around a bit."

Hollywood's Adolph Zukor was said to have offered a trifling $30,000 for movie rights to a Kaufman play. The playwright sent back a telegram offering Zukor $40,000 for Paramount.

Ruth Gordon once described to G.S.K. a new play in which she was appearing: "In the first scene I'm on the left side of the stage, and the audience has to imagine I'm eating dinner in a crowded restaurant. Then in scene two I run over to the right side of the stage and the audience imagines I'm in my own drawing room."

G.S.K. listened, then mused, "And the second night *you* have to imagine there's an audience out front."

Referring to a belligerent author well known for his social criticism, Kaufman remarked, "He's in the chips now—but most of them seem to have stayed on his shoulders."

Herbert Bayard Swope, who had a penchant for dining at odd hours, called G.S.K. one evening at 9:30 and asked, "What are you doing for dinner tonight?"

"I'm digesting it," Kaufman replied.

As a panelist on the television show "This Is Show Business"—which Kaufman called "This Ain't Show Business"—the playwright was asked to comment on "the value of clothes to a performer."

"Clothes cannot be terribly important," he answered, "because if they were, the Duchess of Windsor would be the greatest performer on any stage today."

One evening on "This Is Show Business," a nonsinging actor from a Broadway musical complained that he never got a chance to sing. Said Kaufman: "Why don't you some night just break out and sing? Who can stop you? You're stronger than Gertrude Lawrence. Just do it. For good measure, sing an Irving Berlin tune and get me a close-up of Mr. Rodgers' face at the time."

Beatrice Kaufman one afternoon met so many friends and relatives—from her native Rochester—on Fifth Avenue that she said to George, "All Rochester must be in New York this week."

"What a fine time to visit Rochester," Kaufman observed.

🕊

G.S.K.'s daughter once informed him that a friend of hers from Vassar had eloped. Kaufman remarked philosophically, "Ah! She put her heart before the course."

🕊

Alexander Woollcott, who collaborated with Kaufman on *The Dark Tower*, told of a rehearsal when one of the players, doomed by his role to enlarge himself with padding, cried out, "I certainly hate to walk out on the stage with a big paunch." There was a moment of embarrassing silence, broken by Kaufman saying gravely, "You have grossly insulted Alexander Woollcott."

🕊

A story has it that a "blue-blooded" guest staying at the Algonquin became overbearing one evening in describing his impressive lineage: "I can trace my family back to the Crusades," he said.

"I had such an ancestor, too," replied Kaufman. "Sir

Roderick Kaufman. He also went on the Crusades—as a spy, of course."

In 1957, deploring the way musical comedies had grown serious and tearful, Kaufman wrote in *The New York Times Magazine:* "A funny thing happened to a musical comedy on its way to the theater the other night. It met a joke. Then, before it realized the audacity of such behavior, it took it along to the theater, and presently there it was in the show."

Serving as director for one of George Oppenheimer's plays, Kaufman suggested a line for a character who was to say he'd never been to Boston: "I went through once but it was closed."

After a game of stud poker at a Thanatopsis session Kaufman raked in his $1,900 winnings and presented a dirge for all winners: "Check and rubber check."

Asked once what he thought of the comedy team of Dean Martin and Jerry Lewis, Kaufman remarked: "Martin and Lewis is a very funny fellow."

On the radio show "Information, Please" George Kaufman, serving as a panelist, failed to answer a single question during the "warm-up" period. Just before broadcast time Clifton Fadiman, the show's monitor, said jokingly to Kaufman, "May I ask what *you* have been doing for the past fifteen minutes?"

Kaufman answered: "You may. I've been listening to 'Information, Please.'"

Punning was one of the more popular verbal amusements with the Round Table group, and G.S.K. was a decided master. Two of the most famous Kaufman puns, reportedly delivered at Thanatopsis sessions, were:

"I fold my tens like the Arabs, and as silently steal away."

"One man's Mede is another man's Persian."

Although Woollcott claimed it was originally his, one of the classic puns attributed to Kaufman dealt with "a cat hospital where they charged $4 a weak purr."

One day at the Round Table, Aleck Woollcott made a remark which George Kaufman felt derided his Jewish ancestry. After defining his position to Woollcott, G.S.K.

got up from his seat and said, "I am now walking away from this table, out of the dining room, and out of this hotel." Then, surveying the group, he spotted Dorothy Parker—who was of both Jewish and Gentile parentage—and added, "And I hope that Mrs. Parker will walk out with me—half way."

Writing for John Crosby's column, Kaufman told the following story: "The effectiveness of radio commercials is debated this way and that, but one young matron of my acquaintance can testify that they make quite an impression. The lady in question was anxious to send her ten-year-old daughter to a summer camp, and was duly filling out a questionnaire. Religion? it asked, and she was about to write Presbyterian when the radio went into a commercial. So she wrote Pepsodent instead. The child was turned down—apparently they didn't want any Pepsodents at that camp. Felt there might be trouble."

One Thanksgiving holiday, the Kaufmans, the Sherwoods, the Rosses, the Herbert Bayard Swopes, the Heywood Brouns, Peggy Pulitzer, Oscar Levant, and others all gathered at the Averell Harrimans. During dinner someone remarked, "What a play this gathering would make!" To which Kaufman agreed, adding that an appropriate title might be "The Upper Depths."

G.S.K. once suggested his own epitaph: "Over my dead body!"

Ring Lardner

RING · LARDNER [1885–1933] *began his literary career as a sports writer, rising to the authorship of a humorous sporting column in the Chicago* Tribune. *"Letters of a Bush-League Ball Player" earned him an early reputation as a humorist, and he soon turned from journalism to writing short stories, collections of which have been published in various editions (e.g.,* You Know Me, Al, How to Write Short Stories, Shut Up! He Explained). *Considered by many to be one of the foremost masters of the American short story, Lardner was particularly adept at handling Western rural dialect. His comic style grew out of the Mark Twain tradition of folk humor— simplified, unassuming, tinged with a strain of bitterness and despair. In the words of F. Scott Fitzgerald, Lardner was "a proud, shy, solemn, shrewd, polite, brave, kind, merciful, honorable man [who] made no enemies . . . and to many millions . . . gave release." Never a willing conversationalist, Lardner often remained silent in public, springing forth with well-timed dry or witty remarks when and if the spirit moved him.*

Ring once sent the following telegram to a friend who was away vacationing: "WHEN ARE YOU COMING BACK AND WHY?"

Before turning successfully to journalism, Lardner held a variety of jobs, including a brief stint with a firm that collected "bad debts." He later observed, commenting on that phrase, "I never heard of a good debt."

Lardner was amused by Henry Ford's famous comment on John D. Rockefeller, "I saw John D. Rockefeller but once. But when I saw that face I knew what made Standard Oil." Lardner himself once observed, "[I] also have seen John D. only once and that was on the golf course at Ormond, too far from him to get a look at his face, but the instant I beheld that stance I knew what made divots."

"Last night President Harding and I attended *The Merry Widow*, but not together."

In an autobiographical spoof, Ring tried his hand at some vaudevillian dialogue:

"One of the traits or characteristics for which [I] have been noted in recent years is dignity, self-possession. Only the other day I was complimented on this by no less a personage than Mr. Charles M. Schwab.

" 'Lardy,' he said in his enchanting Southern drawl, 'you certainly have a lot of poise.'

" 'Yes,' I replied lightly. 'Three are at home and one is away at school.' "

Ring once referred to his prep-school-aged sons as his "four grandsons," explaining to a puzzled acquaintance that they cost him "Four grand a year."

Ring frequently recalled the story of an ex-coroner in St. Paul who wrote an ode to his mother that included this line: "If by perchance the inevitable should come."

President Coolidge's inimitable deadpan personality became a cherished target for the Round Tablers' wit. After his first meeting with Coolidge, Lardner reported to the group that he had told the President a humorous anecdote, adding, "He laughed until you could hear a pin drop."

On a certain baseball player: "Although he is a bad fielder he is also a poor hitter."

Invited to a poker game by Heywood Broun, Lardner said over the telephone, "I can't make it tonight, Heywood, it's my little son's night out and I've got to stay home with the nurse."

"You know you've had a few too many when you come home and find cold scrambled eggs on top of last night's lamb chops."

Lardner was a master of American slang and colloquialism. He once wrote, " 'Never will' and 'won't never' are American. 'Never won't' ain't."

Lardner once visited Paducah to interview Irvin Cobb, later reporting, "Mr. Cobb took me into his library and showed me his books, of which he has a complete set."

On wives:[1]

"They are people whose watch is always a ¼ hr. off either one way or the other. But they wouldn't have no idear what time it was anyway as this daylight savings gets them all balled up."

"They are people that think when the telephone bell rings it is against the law not to answer it."

"They are people who you get invited out somewheres with them and you ask them if they think you ought to shave and they say no, you look all right. But when you get to wherever you are going they ask everybody to please forgive Lute as he didn't have time to shave."

"Wives is people that asks you what time the 12:55 train gets to New York. 'At 1:37,' you tell them. 'How do you know?' they ask."

"A man defending husbands vs. wives, or men vs. women, has got about as much chance as a traffic po-

[1] From *Say It With Oil*, George H. Doran Co., 1923.

liceman trying to stop a mad dog by blowing two whistles."

♨

Humorous stories about a baseball rookie, *You Know Me, Al,* brought Lardner early fame as a writer. So many readers asked him to name the player on whom his caricature was based that he added a footnote to subsequent editions: "The original of Jack Keefe is not a ball player at all, but Jane Addams of Hull House, a former Follies girl."

♨

One evening at the Friars Club a fellow member asked Lardner to read aloud a poem written by the member's brother, twenty years dead. After he finished, Ring asked, "Did he write it before or after he died?"

♨

"Frenchmen drink wine just like we used to drink water before Prohibition."

♨

"They ain't no man or woman liveing that can pick up all their soup from a flat lie useing only a spoon and the result is that from 1/10 to a 1/2 an inch is always left laying in the bottom of the dish which is plane waste as the most economical Jap in the world cannot do nothing with left over soup only throw it in the ash can."[2]

Never a supporter of Prohibition, Lardner waged a series of his own antidrinking campaigns, like the following: "If the penalty for selling honest old beer to minors was $100 fine, why 2 to 14 years in a meat grinder would be mild for a guy that sells "white pop" on the theory that it is a drink."

Lardner once played a round of golf with President Warren Harding. In the clubhouse afterward, the President, who said he had enjoyed the round thoroughly, asked Ring, "Is there anything I can do for you?"

"Yes," Ring answered. "I want to be ambassador to Greece."

"Why do you want to go there?" the President asked.

"Because my wife has grown tired of Great Neck."

Discussing the circumstances under which he composed one of his early books, Ring commented:

[2] From *The Lardner Reader*, ed. Maxwell Geismar, New York, Charles Scribner's Sons, 1963, p. 465.

"The contents of *The Big Town* were written mostly in a furnished house in Greenwich, Connecticut, and the author wishes to thank the rats for staying out of the room while he worked. It was wintertime and the furnished house was a summer cottage, but we didn't realize that when we rented it. Nor, apparently, did the rats."[3]

★

In the words of Harold Ross: "I asked Lardner the other day how he writes his short stories, and he said he wrote a few widely separated words or phrases on a piece of paper and then went back and filled in the spaces."

★

ON HORSES: "Defenders of le Horse will no doubt point to the term 'good, common horse sense,' or the simile 'work like a horse,' as being proof of the beast's virtues, but if a horse has got such good common sense, why do they always have to have a jockey show them the way around a fenced in race track where you couldn't possible go wrong unless you was dumb . . . as for working like a horse, I never met a horse who worked because he thought it was funny. They work for the same reason the rest of us works."[4]

[3] From Preface to *The Big Town*.
[4] *The Lardner Reader*, p. 557.

"He gave her a look that you could have poured on a waffle."

"If he got stewed and fell in the gutter he'd catch a fish."

"Well I happened to be sitting in a card game the other night with 5 others of whom 2 besides myself was gents and at first I kept wondering to myself why was it I felt so happy as I am generally always miserable in a card game on acct. of not having no luck. Well my luck wasn't no better than usual so I had to look for another reason and it finely come to me like a flash. The other 2 gents in the game was also losing their hair."[5]

While *June Moon* (which Ring wrote in collaboration with Kaufman) was having its tryout in Atlantic City, the critics there opined that the play had a great second act, but that the first and third acts needed rewriting. Strolling the boardwalk one day Ring met a friend, who asked, "What are you doing here?"

"I'm down here with an act," Ring answered.

[5] *Ibid.*, p. 655.

At a Thanatopsis session, Aleck Woollcott got into an argument with a visiting player over past military experiences. Aleck, at his nastiest, grew increasingly sarcastic with the other, an ex-infantryman. Finally the visitor shouted at Woollcott, "At least I'm not a writing soldier!"

Addressing the visitor, Lardner then made what was said to be his only remark of the evening: "You sure swept the table that time."

Seated at the bar in a theater district nightclub, Ring was approached by an ostentatious actor-type with a wild, flowing mane. Lardner asked the man, "How do you look when I'm sober?"

Lardner once told a group of fellow writers of a note he had penned to Santa Claus: "Please bring this little Lardner boy a waste basket and don't attach a card saying you hope he will make use of it."

Ask by *Vanity Fair* editor Frank Crowninshield to list qualifications for the ideal woman, Lardner composed the following set of specifications:

1. Lockjaw

2. Hereditary obesity
3. Shortness of breath
4. Falling arches
5. Mechanical engineering
6. Draftsmanship
7. Absolutely fireproof
8. Day and night elevator service
9. Laundry sent out before 8:30 A.M. will be returned the same day.

10. Please report to the management any incivility on part of employees.

In the hospital just before he died, Lardner wrote a parody of O. O. McIntyre's famous gossip column. Affecting the pseudo-casual tone of the name-dropping columnist, Ring let his thoughts and opinions ramble on, seemingly at will:

"Thoughts while strolling: Damon Runyon's feet. Kate Smith, a small-town girl who became nationwide in a big city. Rosamund Pinchot and Theodore Dreiser could pass for twins. Rube Goldberg never wears a hat to bed. There is a striking resemblance between Damon Runyon's feet and Ethel Merman. . . ."

ADVICE TO MARRIED COUPLES: "Both partys should try and talk about subjects that the other is interested in.

They ain't no husband cares a damn if the wash woman that is comeing next wk. goes to a different church than the one that was here last wk. and they's very few wifes cares the same amt. whether Max Baer is going to be the next heavyweight champion, so the idear is that when supper is over and the loveing pair sets down in the liveing room to wait till its polite to go to bed, the husband should ought to insist that they won't be no conversation unlest its about the wash woman and the wife should ought to insist that they won't be no conversation unless its about the next heavyweight champ, and if the both of them insist hard enough they won't be no conversation at all which boarders on the ideal."[6]

ON MARRIAGE: "Pretty near any complaint you make about wives, why it is true they will probably resent it. But I often ask myself the question could I get along without them? And the answer to that is that I got along without none for twenty-five yrs. and never felt better in my life."[7]

ON HISTORY: "It was during the early days of the subway that Emile Zola visited New York and remarked in broken French: 'Why you New Yorkers are like ze little

---

[6] *The Lardner Reader*, p. 463.
[7] *Ibid.*, p. 463.

animals, what you call them, ze moles. You are always burrowing in ze ground.' Horace Greeley was much taken with this comment and made a suggestion that was afterwards put into effect—that the city be divided into burrows, the Burrow of Brooklyn, the Burrow of the Bronx, etc."

ON HISTORY: "In 1900, Robert Fulton invented and tried to introduce the automatic or dial telephone. His invention was turned down, unwillingly, by the phone trust in compliance with a petition from people in the then infantile motion picture industry, who argued that the strain of attempting to learn the alphabet would reek havoc with their Art."

ON PROHIBITION: "I don't believe I am betraying a confidence when I say that there are, in this country, several organizations whose aim is to effect the modification or repeal of the Eighteenth Amendment."

Asked once to comment on how his wife had helped him and his career, Lardner reminisced: "In 1914 or 1915, I think it was July, she cleaned my white shoes. She dusted my typewriter in 1922. Late one night in 1924 we got home from somewhere and I said I was hungry and she gave me a verbal picture of the location of the pantry.

"Another time I quit cigarettes and she felt sorry for me."

Author Clarence Budington Kelland, who lived near the Lardners on Long Island, was awakened by Ring at three o'clock one morning. After inviting him in, Kelland discovered that Ring was in one of his silent moods and desired company itself but not conversation. Kelland fell asleep and was awakened at dawn by Ring tapping him on the shoulder. "I don't want to seem rude," Ring whispered, "but aren't you ever going home?"

ON PROHIBITION (from *The Big Drought*, 1925): "Well they was a lot of people in the U.S. that was in flavor of [Prohibition] and finely congress passed a law making the country dry and the law went into effect about the 20 of Jan. 1920 and the night before it went into effect everybody had a big party on acct. of it being the last chance to get boiled. As these wds. is written the party is just beginning to get good."

Dorothy Parker

DOROTHY (ROTHSCHILD) PARKER [1893–1967], *literary critic, short story and verse writer, started her career as drama critic for* Vanity Fair (*with fellow Round Tablers Robert Benchley and Robert Sherwood*). *A gifted writer of short, humorous prose—her story "Big Blonde" won the O. Henry Prize. She is best remembered for her verse, usually light, witty, and gently mocking in tone. Political-minded and sharing Broun's liberalism, she astonished certain friends when she took a job, for a time, writing for the Marxist magazine* New Masses. *In these writings, she often chided "the gilt and brass of a certain type of American personality, the self-absorbed female snob," and satirized the nineteenth-century ideal of vacuous, idle womanhood. She was called by Alexander Woollcott "a combination of Little Nell and Lady Macbeth." Mrs. Parker's demure appearance belied an acid wit and ready tongue that knew few equals. Among the Round Tablers, she was perhaps the most devastating master of repartee and the verbal put-down.*

Dorothy Parker gave the following advice to a friend whose ailing cat had to be put away; "Try curiosity."

☙

Early in her career Mrs. Parker wrote captions for *Vogue* magazine, later confessing to *Vanity Fair* editor Frank Crowninshield that "fashion would never become a religion" with her. One of the lines that guaranteed her a short-lived apprenticeship as a caption writer read: "Brevity is the soul of Lingerie, as the Petticoat said to the Chemise."

☙

One noon hour at the Round Table, a lady author was congratulating herself on her marital success and extolling the virtues of her mate. "I've kept him for seven years," she concluded with pride. The Round Table group did not share the wife's opinion of her spouse, however, considering him an extremely dull fellow. Mrs. Parker answered the lady's remark: "Don't worry, if you keep him long enough he'll come back in style."

☙

"Excuse me, everybody," Mrs. Parker said one day, rising from her chair at the Round Table, "I have to go to the bathroom." Then, after a brief pause: "I really have to telephone, but I'm too embarrassed to say so."

Mrs. Parker once collided with Clare Boothe Luce in a doorway. "Age before beauty," cracked Mrs. Luce.

"Pearls before swine," said Mrs. Parker, gliding through the door.

"Men don't like nobility in women. Not any men. I suppose it is because the men like to have the copyrights on nobility—if there is going to be anything like that in a relationship."

"It's a terrible thing to say, but I can't think of good women writers. Of course, calling them women writers is their ruin; they begin to think of themselves that way."

"Woman's life must be wrapped up in a man, and the cleverest woman on earth is the biggest fool with a man."

Reporting on a Yale prom, Mrs. Parker said, "If all those sweet young things present were laid end to end, I wouldn't be at all surprised."

"His voice was as intimate as the rustle of sheets."

Reviewing a book on science, Mrs. Parker wrote, "It was written without fear and without research."

Commenting on Lucius Beebe's *Shoot If You Must,* Mrs. Parker declared, "This must be a gift book. That is to say, a book which you wouldn't take on any other terms."

Describing a guest at one of her parties: "That woman speaks eighteen languages and can't say 'No' in any of them."

When Mary Sherwood—wife of the playwright—gave birth to a child (an event that most of the Round Tablers felt she had made too much of), Mrs. Parker cabled her: "DEAR MARY, WE ALL KNEW YOU HAD IT IN YOU."

Mrs. Parker once said of a Londoner who spoke in clipped accents: "Whenever I meet one of those Britishers I feel as if I have a papoose on my back."

Sitting next to a table of visiting Midwestern governors in a New York nightclub, Mrs. Parker summed up their conversation: "Sounds like over-written Sinclair Lewis."

"How can you tell?" asked Mrs. Parker on hearing that Calvin Coolidge was dead.

Somerset Maugham, seated next to Mrs. Parker at a party, asked her to write a poem for him. Mrs. Parker wrote:

> Higgledy piggledy, my white hen;
> She lays eggs for gentlemen.

Mr. Maugham commented that he liked those lines. With a cool smile Mrs. Parker quickly added two more:

> You cannot persuade her with gun or lariat
> To come across for the proletariat.

Asked if she had enjoyed a cocktail party at which she had been seen, Mrs. Parker said, "Enjoyed it! One more drink and I'd have been under the host."

Mrs. Parker co-authored with Elmer Rice a play titled *Close Harmony*, which flopped after a very brief run. The night it closed Mrs. Parker wired Robert Benchley: "CLOSE HARMONY DID A COOL NINETY DOLLARS AT THE MATINEE STOP ASK THE BOYS IN THE BACK ROOM WHAT THEY WILL HAVE."

"A girl's best frend is her mutter."

Book review: "This is not a novel to be tossed aside lightly. It should be thrown with great force."

Mrs. Parker remarked, at the reception following her remarriage to Alan Campbell: "People who haven't talked to each other in years are on speaking terms again today—including the bride and groom."

As a writer of book reviews, Mrs. Parker experienced many tedious moments, but her most difficult times came when forced to review novels of "sensational" appeal. On this occupational hazard she once commented: "It's not just 'Lady Chatterley's Husbands.' It's that, after this week's course of reading, I'm good and through with the whole matter of sex. I say it's spinach, and I say to hell with it!"

Dorothy Parker was once informed that a female acquaintance had broken her leg while vacationing in London. "Probably sliding down a barrister," Mrs. Parker suggested.

Of Ford Madox Ford's *The Last Post*, Mrs. Parker wrote: "I have been faithful to my duty, in my fashion. I have read the book."

A friend who had attended a party with Mrs. Parker described their hostess, a loquacious, domineering woman, as "outspoken." "Outspoken by whom?" Mrs. Parker asked.

At a dinner party Mrs. Parker joined a group of guests who were delighting in the routine of a slightly clownish wit. Her date, a snobbish young man, derided the performer. "I'm afraid I can't join in the merriment," he said, "I can't bear fools."

"That's queer," said Mrs. Parker. "Your mother could."

Mrs. Parker once complained to friends that her dog had caught a "social disease" from using "a public lamppost."

"I met a strange fellow up in Canada, the tallest man I ever saw, with a scar on his forehead. I asked him how he got the scar, and he said he must have hit himself. I asked him how he could reach so high. He said he guessed he must have stood on a chair."

Margot Asquith, an English countess, published an autobiography which filled four large volumes, a literary endeavor that Dorothy Parker found tedious and over-personalized. Mrs. Parker predicted: "The affair between Margot Asquith and Margot Asquith will live as one of the prettiest love stories in all literature."

On Margot Asquith's book *Lay Sermons,* Mrs. Parker commented: *"Lay Sermons* is a naïve and an annoying and an unimportant book. The author says 'I am not sure that my ultimate choice for the name of this modest work is altogether happy.' Happier I think it would have been if, instead of the word 'Sermons,' she had selected the word 'off.' "

" 'Daddy, what's an optimist?' said Pat to Mike while they were walking down the street together one day. 'One who thought Margot Asquith wasn't going to write any more,' replied the absentminded professor, as he wound up the cat and put the clock out."

After addressing an antiwar poem called "Hate Song" to all men, Mrs. Parker wrote of herself:

> But I, despite expert advice
> Keep doing things I think are nice,
> And though to good I never come—
> Inseparable my nose and thumb.

At the 92nd birthday celebration of Negro leader W. E. B. Du Bois, guest Dorothy Parker was seated next to the venerable old gentleman. Part of the entertainment was an African spear dance; as the dance increased in intensity and the spears jabbed back and forth with less and less precision in front of Mr. Du Bois, Dorothy Parker leaned over to him and said, "Watch out, mate, or you'll never see 93."

Robert Sherwood was frequently the butt of quips and jokes concerning his towering height. After a prolonged spell of Sherwood absences from the Round Table, Dorothy Parker wired him: "WE'VE TURNED DOWN A VACANT STEPLADDER FOR YOU."

Asked why she had named her pet canary Onan, Mrs. Parker explained, "Because it spills its seed upon the ground."

One evening Mrs. Parker arrived late to a party given by Herbert Baynard Swope, and observed the guests engaged in some sort of group amusement. Swope explained that the guests were "ducking for apples," and Mrs. Parker reflected, "There, but for a typographical error, is the story of my life."

On being shown a plush Manhattan apartment by a real estate agent, Mrs. Parker complained, "Oh, dear, that's much too big. All I need is room enough to lay a hat and a few friends."

Informed that the world-famous she-male Christine Jorgensen was planning a trip to the States in order to visit her mother, Mrs. Parker inquired: "And what sex, may I ask, is the mother?"

Playing "I-Can-Give-You-A-Sentence" with the word horticulture, Mrs. Parker said: "You may lead a whore to culture, but you can't make her think."

Reviewing actress Billie Burke in Maugham's play *Caesar's Wife*, Mrs. Parker wrote: "Miss Burke is at her best in her more serious moments; in her desire to convey the girlishness of the character, she plays her lighter scenes rather as if she were giving an impersonation of Eva Tanguay."

Mrs. Parker once said of a Katharine Hepburn performance: "She ran the whole gamut of emotions, from A to
B."

Of the play *House Beautiful* Mrs. Parker commented:
"*House Beautiful* is the play lousy."

Leonard Lyons once asked Dorothy Parker to describe
her Bucks County farm in two words, to which she replied, "Want it?"

Of her poetry Mrs. Parker said, "I was following in the
exquisite footsteps of Miss Edna St. Vincent Millay, unhappily in my own horrible sneakers."

Mrs. Parker taught for a time at Los Angeles State College, where she found the students very "narrow." When
reading Steinbeck's *The Grapes of Wrath*, for example,
the students felt that the book was too dirty. "But then
Steinbeck won the Nobel Prize," Mrs. Parker recalled.
"After that they behaved as if they had given it to
him."

Sitting next to a middle-aged woman acquaintance at a supper engagement, Mrs. Parker became annoyed at her neighbor's constant overattentiveness—amounting to outright ogling—to an embarrassed Army colonel seated opposite them. "It's his uniform; I just love soldiers," the lady remarked.

"Yes," Mrs. Parker agreed, "you have in every war."

Dorothy Parker and Beatrice Kaufman once visited Heywood Broun's home (Heywood's house clearly reflected his well-known sloppiness) and Beatrice reportedly discovered a couple of yellowed, worn-out toothbrushes hanging in the bathroom. Shocked, Mrs. Kaufman asked, "What on earth are these things?"

"Don't you recognize them?" said Mrs. Parker, "those are the broomsticks the witches ride every Halloween."

"Most good women are hidden treasures who are only safe because nobody looks for them."

Mrs. Parker, who did not relish playing the celebrity, was confronted at a party by a woman who inquired, "Are you Dorothy Parker?"

"Yes, do you mind?" Mrs. Parker answered.

Speaking of Hollywood money, Mrs. Parker said: "It's congealed snow; it melts in your hand."

Mrs. Parker once advised a young reactionary: "Stop looking at the world through rose-colored bifocals."

Told that Clare Boothe Luce was invariably kind to her inferiors, Mrs. Parker asked, "And where does she find them?"

"The reading of *Dawn* [by Theodore Dreiser] is a strain upon many parts, but the worst wear and tear fall upon the forearms."

"Wit has truth in it; wisecracking is simply calisthenics with words."

"You can't teach an old dogma new tricks."

Discussing a job with a prospective employer, Mrs. Parker explained, "Salary is no object; I want only enough to keep body and soul apart."

On her seventieth birthday Dorothy Parker said: "If I had any decency, I'd be dead. Most of my friends are."

Of her poetry: "I'm always chasing Rimbauds."

Expressing her opinion of a writer whom she considered overpraised, Mrs. Parker said, "He's a writer for the ages —for the ages of four to eight."

Dorothy Parker once requested that her epitaph read: "Excuse my dust." Later she suggested another reading: "This is on me."

"A list of our authors who have made themselves most beloved and, therefore, most comfortable financially, shows that it is our national joy to mistake for the first-rate, the fecund rate."

A young playwright, who Mrs. Parker felt had been copying her themes, described his most recent play to her as follows: "It's hard to say—except that it's a play against all isms."

Mrs. Parker added, "Except plagiarism."

Speaking of a stage director with whom she had never gotten along, Mrs. Parker's comment was: "A cad. A card-carrying cad."

Once, while convalescing in the hospital, Mrs. Parker wished to dictate letters to her secretary. Pushing a button marked "Nurse," she said: "This should assure us of at least forty-five minutes of undisturbed privacy."

Two full-length plays were written about the fascinating character of Dorothy Parker—one by George Oppenheimer, the other by Ruth Gordon. Mrs. Parker once commented, "Now, I suppose, if I ever wrote a play about myself I'd be sued for plagiarism."

Alexander Woollcott

ALEXANDER WOOLLCOTT [1887–1943], *literary and drama critic and essayist, was a self-styled arbiter of taste and fashion, especially in literature and theater. His collected works were published under the titles* Long Long Ago *and* While Rome Burns. *He became active in drama not only as critic but as parttime actor (*e.g., The Man Who Came to Dinner) *and playwright (*e.g., The Dark Tower *written with George Kaufman). Large, round, and bespectacled, Woollcott possessed a host of eccentricities and a temperamental nature. Called by Ben Hecht "a persnickety fellow with more fizz than brain" and named by Thurber "Old Vitriol and Violets," he was the butt of countless jokes at the Round Table. He alternated between joking back and turning harmless jests into serious quarrels. Though a bachelor, Woollcott was never a loner. In the words of his constant friend, Harpo Marx, "He loved the pure existence part of living, the yapping, scrapping, laughing, eating, romping, exploring the world part of it—but never, sad to say, the* *intimate, sexual part of it." He had a cutting, sarcastic wit which, when controlled, could be extremely poignant and entertaining. From 1929 to 1940, he became well known as a radio commentator with his own show.*

On a voyage to Shanghai, Alexander Woollcott, at his heftiest, was interviewed by ship-news reporters: "I wish emphatically to deny," said Aleck, pointing to his outsized paunch, "that all rickshaw boys plan to go on strike when I arrive in China."

Aleck Woollcott once joined Corey Ford at the Ritz Men's Bar and informed him, "Ford, I plan to spend three days at your house in New Hampshire next week." Not overly pleased at the prospect of hosting such a demanding guest, Ford uttered a meek "That will be swell."

"I'll be the judge of that," Woollcott warned.

On the occasion of George and Beatrice Kaufman's fifth wedding anniversary Woollcott wrote them, "I have been looking around for an appropriate wooden gift, and am pleased hereby to present you with Elsie Ferguson's performance in her new play."

After the first stage performance of *Our Town*, the producers reportedly found Woollcott—a true sentimentalist—sobbing openly on a fire escape in the theater alley. "Pardon me, Mr. Woollcott," one of them asked, "will you endorse the play?"

Rising, Aleck replied, "Certainly not! It doesn't need it. I'd as soon think of endorsing the Twenty-third Psalm."

One evening Woollcott met painter Neysa McMein at a party where she was dressed in a shimmering gown hung with spangles. "Why, Neysa," Aleck said, "you're scrofulous with mica."

Ever conscious of his weight problem, Woollcott installed a steam cabinet at his "Wit's End" home on the East River. The cabinet had a large window in front, through which an outsider could easily see anyone sitting inside. One afternoon Peggy Pulitzer, while a guest at Woollcott's, wandered by the cabinet and beheld Aleck's stark-naked form. Later she advised him, "You should cover that window with an organdy curtain." Woollcott corrected the lady's phrasing, however: "Curtain de organ."

"You," Woollcott once said to a woman guest, in a roundabout insult, "are married to a cuckold."

🚩

Not one for strenuous exercise or sports, Aleck once witnessed a professional ski meet at Sun Valley. Taking out his memo pad, he wrote; "Remind self never to go skiing."

🚩

While residing at a Manhattan hotel, Mr. Woollcott received a call from the desk clerk, informing him that actress Ina Claire was downstairs.

"Send her up," Woollcott said.

"I can't, sir," the clerk said. "She has a dog."

"Either Miss Claire's dog comes up or I'm coming down," Woollcott warned, adding, "I'm in my pajamas."

Miss Claire's dog came up.

🚩

Aleck once said of his friend *New Yorker* editor Harold Ross: "He looks like a dishonest Abe Lincoln."

🚩

Woollcott was known for keeping a coterie of "favored" intimates whose personal and public lives he did his best to run. Each year he made a point of sending out the following letter to twenty or so of such friends: "An-other milestone in American literature is approaching. January 19th is my birthday, in case a sudden flood of sentiment should seek expression in gifts of cash or certified checks."

Dorothy Parker's second husband, Alan Campbell, once gave Aleck's name as a reference when opening a charge account at Wanamaker's. Woollcott obliged:

> Gentlemen:
>
> Mr. Alan Campbell, the present husband of Dorothy Parker, has given my name as a reference in his attempt to open an account at your store. I hope that you will extend this credit to him. Surely Dorothy Parker's position in American letters is such as to make shameful the petty refusals which she and Alan have encountered at many hotels, restaurants and department stores. What if you never get paid? Why shouldn't you stand your share of the expense?"

On the stock market: "A broker is a man who runs your fortune into a shoestring."

At a Hamilton college class reunion Aleck was approached by a man who said to him: "Hello, Alex! You remember me, don't you?"

"I can't remember your name," said Woollcott, "but don't tell me."

᎗

Woollcott, in his own backhanded way, once came to the defense of his friend Michael Arlen: "Arlen, for all his reputation, is not a bounder. He is every other inch a gentleman."

᎗

Reviewing a small, decidedly inferior volume of poetry written by a woman and entitled *And I Shall Make Music,* Woollcott wrote for *The New Yorker,* "Not on my carpet, lady!"

᎗

Because of his uncompromising, often caustic drama criticisms Woollcott was barred from Shubert theaters, an event that threatened his career as a professional critic. Through the support of *The New York Times,* for which he wrote his reviews, Woollcott won his battle against the Shuberts, and at the same time received extensive personal publicity. In the aftermath of the incident, Aleck confided to a friend, "They threw me out, and now I'm basking in the fierce white light that beats upon the thrown."

A friend who had been out of town during Aleck's battle with the Shuberts asked, upon returning, "How did that scrap with the Shuberts come out?"

"Oh," said Woollcott, "that all went up in smoke."

"How do you mean, smoke?"

Woolcott gloated: "Jake Shubert sent me a box of cigars for Christmas."

Woollcott enjoyed a close friendship with Eleanor and Franklin D. Roosevelt, and occasionally visited them at the White House. In a letter to Mrs. Roosevelt, the purpose of which was to solicit the First Lady's hospitality for an approaching vacation, he wrote: "I would like to come for a week or so. If you haven't room for me, there are plenty of other places for me to go. I prefer yours."

While in Washington during the run of *The Man Who Came to Dinner*, Aleck resided at the White House. He later advised Ethel Barrymore to seek similar accommodations when in that city, assuring her, "Mrs. Roosevelt runs the best theatrical boardinghouse in Washington."

One snowy winter morning Harpo Marx telephoned Aleck to say he would come by to take him for a sleigh-ride. After expressing annoyance at being awakened, Woollcott warmed slightly to the idea and said: "A splendiferous thought! I shall be waiting for you in front of the Gotham to come jingling up in your troika. You'll know me by my white beard and the white fur trimming on my red suit. I'm fat and jolly and tend to go around saying 'Ho! Ho! Ho!' to little children. Meanwhile, if you don't mind, I'm going back to beddy-bye. God bless you and keep you safe from anything as dangerous as knowledge."[1]

The Round Table crowd was often accused of professional log-rolling and back-scratching, although the members themseves felt such accusations were unjust. On the occasion of F.P.A.'s harsh review of a Heywood Broun novel, Woollcott remarked, "You can see Frank's scratches on Heywood's back yet."

While writing for *The New Yorker*, Aleck often created difficulties for the editors because of his fondness for off-color anecdotes and phrases. When one of his pieces was rejected for being "too graphic," Woollcott sent a note to the responsible editor: "I want to take this up with the

[1] From *Harpo Speaks*, Bernard Geis Associates, 1961.

proper person and I've always considered you the properest person I know."

🏴

After one of his frequent misunderstandings with *New Yorker* editor Harold Ross, Aleck sent Ross a letter, which included this message: "I think your slogan 'Liberty or Death' is splendid and whichever one you decide on will be all right with me."

🏴

Ross once made a direct appeal to Woollcott to delete a line of copy in order to save *The New Yorker*'s editorial face. Aleck wired Ross: "Sorry I can't save your face if only for some museum."

🏴

Referring to the ill fate of *The Dark Tower*, a play he had written in collaboration with George Kaufman, Woollcott stressed that "it was a tremendous success except for the minor detail that people wouldn't come to see it."

🏴

Woollcott's acting debut was an amateur performance in which he played a scene from *Henry VIII* with Madge

Kennedy before an audience which included Irving Berlin, Helen Hayes, Mrs. Fiske, Alfred Lunt, and Lynn Fontanne. When the curtain opened, revealing Aleck as Henry VIII the audience began a hissing that lasted a full five minutes. As he made his exit Woollcott was heard muttering, "How unpopular Madge Kennedy must be."

Referring to his poodle Duchess, to which he had a strong attachment, Woollcott said: "Considered as a one-man dog, she's a flop. In her fidelity to me, she's a little too much like that girl in France who was true to the 26th Infantry."

Woollcott's letters, like his conversation, varied in tone from the formal and literary to the jocular and sarcastic. In this portion of a letter to his young protégé, Charles Lederer, Aleck seems to have controlled his wit to achieve what reads like a parody of a Browning monologue:

> I have seen so many earls and countesses lately that a glimpse of one so ignobly born as yourself would be refreshing. Have seen nothing of dear Lady Cavendish, who once sat on this old knee. But that was when she was Adele Astaire. I understand she gets along famously with her mother-in-law, the Duchess of Devon-

shire. Has the Duchess saying "Oke" already. Then I suppose I should tell you about Lord Redding's recent marriage to a woman some forty years younger than himself. The London *Times* account of the wedding ended, unfortunately, with this sentence: "The bridegroom's gift to the bride was an antique pendant."[2]

While traveling in the Orient, Woollcott kept up an occasional correspondence with Beatrice Kaufman (G.S.K.'s wife), with whom he had a warm friendship. The closing of one letter read:

> I'm off to Osaka now to see the marionettes and a few good temples. Yesterday I saw a fervent Japanese gentleman standing in the frosty twilight under a sacred waterfall. He wore a suit of tasteful underwear and prayed aloud with chattering teeth for the good of his immortal soul.
>
> Hoping you will soon take similar measures, I remain
>
> Yours respectfully,
A. WOOLLCOTT[3]

Aleck's achievement as a loquacious, one-way conversationalist was matched by none, however glib and outgoing his Round Table colleagues might be. He once

[2] From *The Letters of Alexander Woollcott*, eds. Beatrice Kaufman and Joseph Hennessy, Viking Press, 1944.
[3] *Ibid.*, p. 89.

confessed to a friend, "One day I shall probably talk myself to death," adding philosophically, "Those who live by the word shall perish by the word."

One of Woollcott's closest male-female relationships was with painter Neysa McMein, an affair that spanned several years but never developed beyond warm affection. Aleck once informed Neysa: "I'm thinking of writing the story of our life together. The title is already settled."

"What is it?" the lady asked.

"Under Separate Cover."

Woollcott once tried to persuade Moss Hart to drive him to Newark, where he was to deliver a lecture. Hart said Yes, on condition that Woollcott let him sit next to him on the speakers' platform. (Moss explained that he had once clerked in a Newark bookstore, and now wanted to show them he was a big shot.) At the end of his lecture, Woollcott stated: "I usually have a question period at this time but tonight we'll dispense with it. I'm sure you'd all want to know the same thing: Who is this foolish-looking young man seated here on the platform with me?" Woollcott then marched abruptly from the stage, leaving Moss to find his own way off.

On his first visit to Moss Hart's Bucks County estate, Woollcott wrote in the guest book: "This is to certify that on my first visit to Moss Hart's house I had one of the most unpleasant times I ever spent."

In a letter to humorist Frank Sullivan, Woollcott related the following: "I thought you would like to hear about the telegram just sent by the printers on a small-town Connecticut newspaper to the foreman of the composing room on the occasion of his marriage. It consisted of one word—'Stet!' "[4]

In a note to Alfred Lunt, in 1931, Woollcott wrote: "When your grandchildren (on whom you have not yet made a really effective start) gather at your rheumatic knees and ask you what you did during the great depression, you can tell them that you played *Reunion in Vienna* to crowded houses, and enjoyed the whole depression enormously."[5]

Aleck was once toastmaster at a Theatre Guild dinner, the occasion being to raise money for new Gobelin

[4] *Ibid.*, p. 198.
[5] *Ibid.*, p. 103.

tapestries for its playhouse. Woollcott began his remarks with, "Those Gobelins are going to get you if you don't watch out."

🎬

Harpo Marx once arrived at Woollcott's Lake Bomoseen home in a broken-down Model-T Ford. "What do you call that?" Woollcott exclaimed as he regarded the automobile.

"This is my town car," Harpo explained.

"What was the town?" asked Woollcott. "Pompeii?"

🎬

Struggling to pacify the "head of protocol" at a Paris casino, after his companion Harpo Marx had distressed the gentleman with a few good-natured antics, Aleck turned to Harpo and asked, "How can I explain you? . . . There's no French word for 'boob.' "

🎬

Actress Margalo Gilmore once brought a young actor friend to the Round Table for the express purpose of meeting Aleck Woollcott, whom the young man greatly admired. Somehow sensing Miss Gilmore's intentions, Aleck took a seat at the opposite end of the table. When Miss Gilmore finally got an opportunity to introduce them, she told Aleck that the lad was a fan of everything he had written. "Oh," said Woollcott, not bothering to look up, "can he read?"

In an attempt to capture Dorothy Parker's unique personality, which somehow balanced a childlike innocence with a jaded sophistication, Woollcott called her "a combination of Little Nell and Lady Macbeth."

Shortly before his death, Aleck said to actress Dorothy Gish: "Doctors want to keep you alive. I want to *live*."

"The people of Germany are just as responsible for Hitler as the people of Chicago are for the Chicago *Tribune*."

REGARDING SCHOOL: "Personally, I was the teacher's-pet type, and couldn't pass a school without pausing to matriculate."

"I went to one academy or another for 17 mortal years. And never late once. One day last summer I rather boasted of the record. There were three of us swimming slowly across the lake and I just happened to mention that in seventeen years I was never once late at school. I shall always remember how this simple statement of fact affected my companions. They tried to drown me."

Woollcott was an old Hamilton College classmate and lifelong friend of Harry Kean Yuan, son of Yuan Shih-Kai, president of China from 1912 to 1916. Harry was expelled from Hamilton for throwing rocks through his classroom windows. He subsequently enrolled at Colgate University, which Aleck later described gloatingly as "an institution maintained for benefit of persons expelled from Hamilton."

Kaufman and Hart collaborated in the writing of *The Man Who Came to Dinner*, a Broadway hit in which the leading character, Sheridan Whiteside, was based on the more poisonous characteristics of the Woollcott personality. In a curtain speech, after playing the Whiteside role himself, Woollcott commented, "It's not true that the role of the obnoxious Sheridan Whiteside was patterned after me. Whiteside is merely a composite of the better qualities of the play's two authors."

Reviewing a show in which both the plot and the two starring performers seemed to him soapy and weak, Woollcott wrote two lines: "In the first act *she* becomes a lady. In the second act *he* becomes a lady."

In 1931, Woollcott disclosed, "This year I've done two things I wanted to do—go to Peking, and act in a play. Next year I want to go to Russia and try umbrella mending."

In a review of an ill-fated Broadway opening, Woollcott suggested that the leading man "should have been gently but firmly shot at sunrise."

"All the things I really like to do are either immoral, illegal, or fattening."

One of Woollcott's favorite "mystifying" anecdotes: "Three men sit down to a bottle of brandy and divide it equally between them. When they have finished the bottle one of them leaves the room, and the other two try to guess who left."

ON GAMBLING: "My doctor forbids me to play unless I win."

⚜

Russel Crouse once showed up at a "Wit's End" party looking rather flamboyant in a bright, multicolored sports shirt. Aleck greeted him, announcing to the guests already present, "What I admire most about Crouse is his loyalty. Here he is, a busy author and columnist and playwright, and still he takes time to go all the way back to that little Army and Navy store in Skaneatles, New York, to buy his shirts."

⚜

"My friends will tell you that Woollcott is a nasty old snipe. Don't believe them. Woollcott's friends are a pack of simps who move their lips when they read."

⚜

In a letter to a friend whom he had offended publicly, Woollcott wrote—when he had decided it was time to make up: "I've tried by tender and conscientious nursing to keep my grudge against you alive, but I find it has died on me."

⚜

A self-portrait which reportedly hung in Woollcott's bathroom depicted him sitting on a toilet, the caption reading, "Laxation and Relaxation."

Aleck had scant praise for Hollywood, although the promise of big, easy money lured him into an occasional film. On this subject he remarked: "When I was a freshman at Hamilton I was thrown into the college fount. In the early days of the last war, I had to take care of the bedpans in an Army hospital. But never have I been so humiliated as on my few appearances in the movies."

Woollcott achieved varying degrees of success as a radio commentator, and seemed to take the position seriously. With customary disdain for the general public, however, Aleck commented that radio listeners would be content to hear "the multiplication table if broadcast with sufficient emotion."

Heywood Broun once complained over lunch that current writers were overusing the word "wistful," thus turning it into a chiché. "If they have to be wistful," he said,"why can't they get a book of synonyms and look up a good clean name for it?"

Aleck, who was himself partial to using the word, said to Broun, "Coming from one who, during his entire adult life, has bumped along on the flat wheel of wistfulness, I find this capsule critique ill-advised."

As theater critic for the New York *World*, Woollcott often had no more than twenty minutes to turn out copy on a play he was reviewing. Concerning this nerve-racking and, in his opinion, absurd pressure, he remarked, "It was like engaging Balto to rush a relief supply of macaroons to Nome."

When Beatrice Kaufman gave Woollcott as a reference to the school in which she was enrolling her daughter, she received what at first she took for a carbon copy of Woollcott's letter to the headmistress: "I implore you to accept this unfortunate child and remove her from her shocking environment. . . ." (The letter reportedly went on to describe the fictitious nightly orgies that took place in the Kaufman home.)

A women's club group once presented a citation to Woollcott, who accepted it with a humble bow. "Only a bow?" the chairman chided. "Won't you say just one word?"

Woollcott relented, addressed this group with a formal stare, and uttered one word: "Coo."

Robert Sherwood

Completing the Circle

THE SUPPORTING CAST of *Round Tablers is composed of various celebrities, many of them wits in their own right, others of them professional humorists who, while not constant Algonquin lunchers, nonetheless deserve representation as "fringe" members of the group. The three "regulars" who will be featured in the following pages are novelist Edna Ferber, playwright Robert Sherwood, and* New Yorker *editor Harold Ross.*

Edna Ferber

Preparing to leave for Europe one summer, Edna Ferber confided to interviewers, "I want to be alone on this trip. I don't expect to talk to a man or woman—just Aleck Woollcott."

During an interview, a reporter kept stressing the full scope and epic qualities of some of Miss Ferber's novels, for example, *Ice Palace*. "The canvas is probably rather big," Miss Ferber conceded. "I don't do miniatures."

Growing tired of what she considered Aleck Woollcott's "professional waspism," Miss Ferber dubbed him "the New Jersey Nero who mistakes his pinafore for a toga."

Speaking about reviewers who seemed unable to render honest, objective critiques on the works of such writers as had won the Nobel Prize, Miss Ferber described them as "awestruck by the Nobelity."

After writing *Ice Palace*, which required extensive travel and research, Miss Ferber said she was so tired of traveling that her next novel would be a "stark, red-hot love story about two people in a telephone booth," entitled *But, Operator, I Did Drop My Dime*.

In California, Miss Ferber was introduced to Tess Slesinger, a young lady writer whose work was often said to imitate that of Dorothy Parker. A reported coolness developed between the two. Later, when Miss Ferber was ready to return to New York, a group of Hollywood writers—including Miss Slesinger—went to the depot to see her off. Before leaving, Miss Ferber wandered over to the book counter and asked the salesman, "Where's my book?" The younger authoress also inquired, "And where's my book?" Miss Ferber reached for a copy of Dorothy Parker's *Enough Rope* and said: "Here it is."

The writer Louis Bromfield was known as a cosmopolitan, sophisticated, and very pleasant conversationalist. At one point during his career, however, he fell in love with the earth and took up farming. His monologues, as a result, often spanned the gap between high society and life on the farm so freely that the Round Tablers found it annoying, if not pretentious. One day, after Bromfield had switched his talk from vacationing on the Riviera to what he fed his pigs, Miss Ferber said, "For godsakes, Louis, brush the caviar off your blue jeans."

Miss Ferber, who was fond of wearing tailored suits, showed up at the Round Table one afternoon sporting a new suit similar to one Noël Coward was wearing. "You look almost like a man," Coward said as he greeted her.

"So," Miss Ferber replied, "do you."

While collaborating on their play *The Royal Family*, Edna Ferber and George Kaufman often worked in Miss Ferber's suite at the Algonquin. One midnight a new and conscientious desk clerk telephoned the suite and asked, "I beg your pardon, Miss Ferber, but is there a gentleman in your room?"

"I don't know," Miss Ferber replied. "Wait a minute and I'll ask him."

Miss Ferber, who held a lifelong ambition to be a stage actress, admitted in her autobiography, "To this day I regard myself as a blighted Bernhardt."

Edna Ferber sent the following letter to Harold Ross of *The New Yorker* after the magazine had reviewed a movie based on a Ferber novel: "Will you kindly inform the moron who runs your motion picture department that I did not write the movie entitled *Classified?* Neither did I write any of its wisecracking titles. Also inform him that Moses did not write the motion picture entitled *The Ten Commandments.*"

Dining on chicken hash at the Colony in New York, Miss Ferber remarked, "I find it strangely decadent to order *hash* in the most expensive restaurant in New York. It means we've come full circle, in a way."

"Being an old maid is like death by drowning, a really delightful sensation after you cease to struggle."

Robert E. Sherwood

Robert Sherwood, who at one time served as speech-writer to Franklin D. Roosevelt, was invited to dinner at the White House, the evening's highlight being a special film presentation of his play *Abe Lincoln in Illinois*. Sherwood's brother Arthur—a staunch Republican—asked Robert to bring him a souvenir. "What would you like," asked the playwright, "his scalp?"

Discussing modern presidential history, Sherwood once stated: "All Coolidge had to do in 1924 was to keep his mean trap shut, to be elected. All Harding had to do in 1920 was repeat 'Avoid foreign entanglements.' All Hoover had to do in 1928 was to endorse Coolidge. All Roosevelt had to do in 1932 was to point to Hoover."

One of the members at a Playwrights' Company meeting remarked that he was "on tenterhooks" as to whether he would succeed in procuring the services of a certain actor for a forthcoming production. Interrupting the speaker, Maxwell Anderson appealed to the group for a definition of the term tenterhooks. Sherwood complied: "They are the upholstery of the anxious seat."

At a meeting of the Playwrights' Company a foreign manuscript came under discussion in which the author's meaning was cloaked in symbolism and the general tone abstruse. Sherwood commented drily, "I prefer the plays of Robert Emmet Sherwood. He hasn't got much to say but at least he does not try to say anything else."

Sitting down to a Thanatopsis poker game at the Algonquin, the playwright punned, "Only the brave *chemin de fer*."

As a movie reviewer for *Life*, Sherwood once commented on the cowboy hero Tom Mix: "They say he rides like part of the horse, but they don't say what part."

While writing speeches for an F.D.R. campaign, Sherwood accompanied the President to Philadelphia, where, after Roosevelt had made what seemed to be a successful address, Sherwood complimented him on his "timing" in delivering certain lines. The President smiled and asked his writer, "Do you think your Alfred Lunt could have done it any better?" "Yes," Sherwood replied, followed by the roar of Roosevelt's laughter.

Sherwood served in the Canadian Black Watch Regiment during World War I (his extreme height kept him out of the U.S. Army). In one of his first letters home, the 6'7" lad wrote, "By no stretch of the imagination can I be called an attractive fellow in kilts, but at least I can say that I'm imposing."

Harold Ross

While editing the *American Legion Weekly* as a young man, Ross received a letter from one of America's foremost short-story writers. Not only were the author's name and address engraved on the letterhead, but laudatory critical quotations as well. Before answering the letter, Ross had a new letterhead engraved on the upper left-hand corner of his own notepaper. It read:

"A fine fellow."
—Alexander Woollcott

"Among those present was Harold Ross."
—F.P.A., New York *World*

On hearing that *Time* editor Henry Luce objected to a profile of himself published in *The New Yorker*—on the grounds that not one nice thing was said about him in the whole piece—Ross told him, "That's what you get for trying to be a baby tycoon."

Aleck Woollcott's personality lent itself so readily to caricature that most of his friends and acquaintances at one time or another tried their hand at capturing his general image. Ross once described him as "a fat duchess with the emotions of a fish."

During the F.D.R.–Thomas Dewey battle for the Presidency, *The New Yorker*, allegedly a neutral weekly, appeared to slant its humor more against Dewey than against Roosevelt. When Ross was chided about this, he replied, "If the GOP's wrote funny stuff we'd print that too."

In the early 1930s, when fiction began growing markedly introspective, Ross commented on the flood of "grim" O'Hara-type stories which he printed but rarely approved of: "If a man in these goddam stories doesn't shoot his wife, he shoots himself."

Ross once stated emphatically to Robert Benchley: "Don't think I'm not incoherent."

Ross once caught Thurber in the act of imitating him, a routine that Thurber often repeated for the entertainment of his office-mates. "What's so funny about me?" Ross demanded, revealing all the gestures Thurber had just finished mimicking. "I don't do anything anybody can imitate."

Marc Connelly

Leaving the Round Table one afternoon, brushing impatiently at some lint a new napkin had left on his suit, Marc Connelly glided by Algonquin owner Frank Case and murmured, "I'm going to have a suit made of lint and see if I can pick me up a blue serge."

Frank Sullivan

On the Round Table: "Admission to this charmed circle is difficult, the reason being that the first and prime requisite is that the candidate must have the price of his lunch."

Returning from a lecture tour, Aleck Woollcott reported to a table of Algonquin lunchers that he had spoken to "ten thousand women in St. Paul."

"What did you tell them," asked Sullivan. "No?"

Receiving an award at a Columbia *Jester** banquet for being the man who had done most for humor writing, Harold Ross, never fond of speech-making, uttered one drawn-out word: "Jesus!" Frank Sullivan, who was seated next to Ross, voiced the following criticism: "Your speech was too long, Ross. I got bored after the first Syllable."

* Humor magazine of Columbia University.

Harpo Marx

For years, Benchley the critic carried on a war with the notorious Broadway hit *Abie's Irish Rose*. Near the close of the play's record run Benchley posted a prize for the best critical comment on the show. Harpo Marx won the contest with his capsule critique: "No worse than a bad cold."

In the spring of 1928, Aleck Woollcott invited Harpo Marx to spend the summer with him on the French Riviera. Harpo refused, protesting, "I can think of forty better places to spend the summer, all of them on Long Island in a hammock."

(An interesting postscript: On Saturday, May 19, Aleck Woollcott, Beatrice Kaufman, novelist Alice Duer Miller, and Harpo sailed for Europe.)

Herman Mankiewicz

Watching his Round Table friends leaving the Algonquin one afternoon (when they were still young and relatively unsuccessful), Herman Mankiewicz (not yet a Hollywood producer) said to Murdock Pemberton, "There goes the greatest collection of unsaleable wit in America."

Mankiewicz once explained to a Round Table audience: "You know, it's hard to hear what a bearded man is saying. He can't speak above a whisker."

Irvin S. Cobb

F.P.A.'s upper extremity, the angular beak-nosed countenance supported by a long, bony neck, once caused humorist Irvin Cobb, on seeing a stuffed moose head, to remark, "My God, they've shot Frank Adams."

Alice Duer Miller

Novelist and Round Table frequenter Alice Duer Miller once paid off a loss at cards to Aleck Woollcott, informing him: "You, sir, are the lowest form of life—a cribbage pimp."

Charles MacArthur

Aleck Woollcott and playwright Charles MacArthur once took a voyage to Europe together. After their ship had been two days at sea, MacArthur emerged onto the deck to join Aleck, confiding to him, "I can't get over the feeling that I'm on a boat."

During a period when Benchley roomed with Charles MacArthur at the Shelton Hotel, MacArthur took a temporary job as a public relations counsel for a mausoleum in New Jersey. As his first promotional campaign, MacArthur convinced the firm that it should establish a "Poet's Corner" and change its name to Fairview Abbey. Next, he decided that the firm should at least try to obtain the bones of Henry Wadsworth Longfellow and inter them in its new Corner. To show his sincere intentions he sent a letter to James Michael Curley, mayor of Boston, saying that Boston had forfeited its right to Longfellow's bones on the grounds that a Longfellow poem—lines from which read, "Life is real! Life is earnest!/And the grave is not the goal"—obviously proved that the poet did not wish to be buried in an ordinary grave, but rather in a crypt, or, best of all, in a Poet's Corner—like the one at Fairview Abbey.

When Curley sent back a sincere reply to the effect that some mistake must have been at the bottom of this action, and that, at any rate, Longfellow was buried in Cambridge, under the present jurisdiction of Mayor Flynn, MacArthur got Benchley to team up with him. The two sat down and made out a series of messages to Curley, including such threats as: THE COUNTRY DEMANDS THE BODY OF HENRY WADSWORTH LONGFELLOW; IF YOU VALUE YOUR JOB YOU WILL FORWARD IT TO ME IMMEDIATELY, and COME CLEAN WITH THAT BODY, and ROLL DEM BONES. Curley made serious attempts at getting warrants for their arrests in New Jersey.

Frank Crowninshield

Frank Crowninshield, *Vanity Fair* editor and Round-Table occasional, once observed with Lardnerian wisdom: "Married men make very poor husbands."

Tallulah Bankhead

Dorothy Parker gave a party one night at the Algonquin, and guest Tallulah Bankhead, slightly inebriated, carried on in a wild, indecorous manner. After Miss Bankhead had been escorted out, Mrs. Parker called in from an adjoining room, "Has Whistler's Mother left yet?"

The next day at lunch Tallulah took out a pocket mirror, examined herself painfully, and said, with a glance at Mrs. Parker, "The less I behave like Whistler's Mother the night before, the more I look like her the morning after."

After sitting through the preview of a strikingly bad movie made by an independent producer, Tallulah observed, "What I don't see is what that producer has got to be independent about."

Attending an unsuccessful revival of the Maeterlink play *Aglavaine and Selysette*, Tallulah Bankhead commented to Aleck Woollcott, "There is less in this than meets the eye."

Paul Robeson

Negro singer Paul Robeson was an occasional guest at Thanatopsis poker games. One Saturday night when

Robeson was present, Herbert Bayard Swope (editor of the New York *World*) happened to ask the group, "Did you fellows know that I have a little Jewish blood?"

"And did you-all know that I got a tinge of the tar-brush?" asked Robeson.

Beatrice Kaufman

Beatrice Kaufman, who held little appreciation for music of any sort, once accompanied Oscar Levant to Carnegie Hall to hear Stokowski conduct Bach's B Minor Mass. While en route to the theater Beatrice realized that they were going to be late and urged her escort, "In heaven's name let's hurry or we'll miss the intermission!"

George Oppenheimer, while an editor at Viking Press, was once assigned to collect material for a question-book called *Ask Me Another*. As a promotional gimmick the editors were advised to first test the questions on various celebrities. Covering the "famous authors" section, Oppenheimer asked Beatrice Kaufman: "Who wrote *The Virginian?*"

"Owen Wister," Beatrice answered.

Oppenheimer's next question read: "Who wrote *The Virginians?*"

Reacting against the gimmicky pattern of the questions, Beatrice answered, "Owens Wisters."

Peggy Wood

Peggy Wood, actress and Round Table frequenter, joined the group one day while Woollcott was discussing the feasibility of reviving *Macbeth* as a Broadway play. Acknowledging the arrival of Miss Wood, Aleck said, "We're discussing the cast. I don't think you'd make a very good Lady Macbeth, do you, Peggy?"

"No, Aleck," she answered. "But you would."

Selected Bibliographies

FRANKLIN P. ADAMS

Answer This One: Questions for Everybody, compiled by F.P.A. and Harry Hansen. New York, E. J. Clode, Inc., 1927.

The Book of Diversion, compiled by F.P.A., Deems Taylor, Jack Bechdolt. New York, Greenberg, Inc., 1925.

By and Large. Garden City, Doubleday, Page & Co., 1914.

Christopher Columbus and Other Patriotic Verses. New York, The Viking Press, 1931.

Column Book of F.P.A. Garden City, Doubleday, Doran & Co., Inc., 1928.

The Diary of Our Own Samuel Pepys. New York, Simon and Schuster, 1935.

FPA Book of Quotations, A New Collection of Famous Sayings. New York, Funk & Wagnalls Co., 1952.

Half a Loaf. Garden City, Doubleday, Page & Co., 1927.

In Cupid's Court (Poems). Evanston, W. S. Lord, 1902.

In Other Words (Poems). Garden City, Doubleday, Page & Co., 1912.

Innocent Merriment, compiled by F.P.A. New York, London, Whittlesey House, McGraw-Hill Book Co., 1942.

The Melancholy Lute: Selected Songs of Thirty Years. New York, The Viking Press, 1936.

Nods and Becks. London, New York, Whittlesey House, McGraw-Hill Book Co., Inc., 1944.

Overset. Garden City, Doubleday, Page & Co., 1922.

So Much Velvet. Garden City, Doubleday, Page & Co., 1924.

So There! Garden City, Doubleday, Page & Co., 1923.

Something Else Again. Garden City, Doubleday, Page & Co., 1920.

Tobogganning on Parnassus. Garden City, Doubleday, Page & Co., 1911.

Weights and Measures. Garden City, Doubleday, Page & Co., 1917.

The World, New York: The Conning Tower Book, edited by F.P.A. New York, Macy-Masius, 1926.

ROBERT BENCHLEY

After 1903—What?, with drawings by Gluyas Williams. New York, London, Harper & Brothers, 1938.

Benchley Beside Himself, with drawings by Gluyas Williams. New York, London, Harper & Brothers, 1943.

Benchley—or Else!, with drawings by Gluyas Williams. New York, Harper, 1947.

The Benchley Roundup: a Selection by Nathaniel Benchley of His Favorites, with drawings by Gluyas Williams. New York, Harper, 1954.

Chips Off the Old Benchley, with an introduction by Frank Sullivan and drawings by Gluyas Williams. New York, Harper, 1949.

The Early Worm, with drawings by Gluyas Williams. New York, H. Holt & Company, 1927.

From Bed to Worse: or, Comforting Thoughts about the Bison. New York, London, Harper & Brothers, 1934.

Inside Benchley, with drawings by Gluyas Williams. New York, London, Harper & Brothers, 1942.

Love Conquers All, with drawings by Gluyas Williams. New York, H. Holt & Company, 1922.

My Ten Years in a Quandary, and How They Grew. New York, London, Harper & Brothers, 1936.

No Poems: or, Around the World Backwards and Sideways. New York, London, Harper & Brothers, 1932.

Of All Things. New York, H. Holt & Company, 1921.

Pluck and Luck, with drawings by Gluyas Williams. New York, H. Holt & Company, 1925.

The "Reel" Benchley: Benchley at His Hilarious Best in Words and Pictures. New York, Wyn, 1950.

The Treasurer's Report, and Other Aspects of Community Singing, with drawings by Gluyas Williams. New York, London, Harper & Brothers, 1930.

20,000 Leagues Under the Sea: or, David Copperfield, with drawings by Gluyas Williams. New York, Henry Holt & Company, 1928.

ABOUT ROBERT BENCHLEY:

Robert Benchley, a Biography, by Nathaniel Benchley. New York, McGraw-Hill, 1955.

HEYWOOD BROUN

The A.E.F., With General Pershing and the American Forces. New York, London, D. Appleton & Co., 1918.

Anthony Comstock, Roundsman of the Lord, by Heywood Broun and Margaret Leech. New York, A. & C. Boni, 1927.

The Boy Grew Older. New York, London, G. P. Putnam's Sons, 1922.

Christians Only, a Study of Prejudice, by Heywood Broun and George Britt. New York, The Vanguard Press, 1931.

Collected Edition of Heywood Broun, compiled by Heywood (Hale) Broun. New York, Harcourt, Brace & Co., 1941.

Gandle Follows His Nose. New York, Boni & Liveright, 1926.

It Seems to Me, 1925–1935. New York, Harcourt, Brace & Co., 1935.

Our Army at the Front. New York, Charles Scribner's Sons, 1918.

Pieces of Hate and Other Enthusiasms. New York, G. H. Doran Co., 1922.

Seeing Things at Night. New York, Harcourt, Brace & Co., 1921.

A Shepherd. New York, William Edwin Rudge, 1926(?).

Sitting on the World. New York, London, G. P. Putnam's Sons, 1924.

The Sun Field. New York, London, G. P. Putnam's Sons, 1923.

ABOUT HEYWOOD BROUN:

Heywood Broun as He Seemed to Us, by John L. Lewis, F.P.A., and others. New York, pub. for Newspaper Guild (Random House), 1940.

GEORGE S. KAUFMAN

Bravo!, a play in three acts, by Kaufman and Edna Ferber. New York, Dramatists Play Service, 1949.

The Butter and Egg Man, a comedy in three acts. New York, French, 1930.

The Dark Tower, melodrama by Kaufman and Alexander Woollcott. New York, Random House, 1934.

Dinner at Eight, a play in three acts, by Kaufman and Edna Ferber. New York, French, 1959.

First Lady, a play in three acts, by Kaufman and Katherine Dayton. New York, Random House, 1935.

June Moon, a comedy by Kaufman and Ring Lardner. New York, London, Charles Scribner's Sons, 1930.

The Land Is Bright, a play in three acts, by Kaufman and Edna Ferber. New York, Dramatists Play Service, 1946.

The Man Who Came to Dinner, by Kaufman and Moss Hart. New York, Random House, 1939.

The Royal Family, a comedy in three acts, by Kaufman and Edna Ferber. New York, French, 1929.

Sister Seraphina's Schiaparelli, a one-act farce. Philadelphia, The Penn Play Co., 1944.

Six Plays by Kaufman and Hart. New York, Modern Library, 1942.

Stage Door, a play in three acts, by Kaufman and Edna Ferber. New York, Dramatists Play Service, 1941.

You Can't Take It With You, by Kaufman and Moss Hart. New York, Dramatists Play Service, 1937.

RING LARDNER

Bib Ballads, with drawings by Fontaine Fox. Chicago, P. F. Volland & Co., 1915.

The Big Town. New York, London, Charles Scribner's Sons, 1925.

The Ecstasy of Owen Muir. London, Cape, 1954.

Gullible's Travels. Chicago, University of Chicago Press, 1965.

First and Last. New York, London, Charles Scribner's Sons, 1934.

The Homecoming of Chas. A. Comiskey, etc. Chicago, The Blakely Printing Co., 1914.

How to Write Short Stories (With Samples). New York, London, Charles Scribner's Sons, 1924.

Lose With a Smile. New York, Charles Scribner's Sons, 1933.

The Love Nest, and Other Stories. New York, Charles Scribner's Sons, 1926.

Own Your Own Home, with drawings by Fontaine Fox. Indianapolis, The Bobbs-Merrill Co., 1919.

The Portable Ring Lardner, edited by Gilbert Seldes. New York, The Viking Press, 1946.

The Real Dope, with drawings by May Wilson Preston and M. L. Blumenthal. Indianapolis, The Bobbs-Merrill Co., 1919.

Ring Lardner's Best Stories. Garden City, Garden City Publishing Co., Inc., 1938.

Roundup, The Stories of Ring W. Lardner. New York, Charles Scribner's Sons, 1929.

Say It With Oil. New York, George H. Doran Co., 1923.

Shut Up, He Explained: A Ring Lardner Selection, edited by Babette Rosmond and Henry Morgan. New York, Scribner, 1962.

The Story of a Wonder Man: being the Autobiography of Ring Lardner, with drawings by Margaret Freeman. New York, Scribner, 1927.

Treat 'em Rough: Letters from Jack the Kaiser Killer, with drawings by Frank Crerie. Indianapolis, The Bobbs-Merrill Co., 1918.

What Of It? New York, London, Charles Scribner's Sons, 1925.

You Know Me Al: A Busher's Letters. New York, George H. Doran Co., 1916.

The Young Immigrunts. Indianapolis, The Bobbs-Merrill Co., 1920.

ABOUT RING LARDNER:

Ring Lardner, a Biography, by Donald Elder. Garden City, Doubleday, 1956.

DOROTHY PARKER

After Such Pleasures. New York, The Viking Press, 1933.

Close Harmony: or, The Lady Next Door, a play in three acts by Dorothy Parker and Elmer Rice. New York, Samuel French; London, French, Ltd., 1929.

Collected Poems: Not So Deep as a Well. New York, The Viking Press, 1936.

The Collected Poetry of Dorothy Parker. New York, The Modern Library, 1944.

Death and Taxes. New York, The Viking Press, 1931.

Dorothy Parker, with an Introduction by W. Somerset Maugham. New York, The Viking Press, 1944.

Enough Rope: Poems by Dorothy Parker. New York, Boni
& Liveright, 1926.

Here Lies. The Collected Stories of Dorothy Parker. New
York, The Viking Press, 1939.

The Ladies of the Corridor, a drama in two acts, by Dorothy
Parker and Arnaud d'Usseau. New York, French, 1954.

Laments for the Living. New York, The Viking Press, 1930.

Sunset Gun; Poems by Dorothy Parker. New York, Boni and
Liveright, 1928.

ALEXANDER WOOLLCOTT

The Command Is Forward, with drawings by Le Roy Bald-
ridge. New York, The Century Co., 1919.

The Dark Tower, a melodrama by A. Woollcott and George
S. Kaufman. New York, Random House, 1934.

Enchanted Aisles. New York, London, G. P. Putnam's Sons,
1924.

Going to Pieces. New York, London, G. P. Putnam's Sons,
1928.

The Good Companions. New York, Privately Printed, 1936.

The Letters of Alexander Woollcott, edited by Beatrice
Kaufman and Joseph Hennessey. New York, The Viking
Press, 1943.

Long, Long Ago. New York, The Viking Press, 1943.

The Portable Woollcott, selected by Joseph Hennessey. New
York, The Viking Press, 1944.

Woollcott's Second Reader, selections by A. Woollcott. New
York, The Viking Press, 1937.

Shouts and Murmurs. London, L. Parsons, 1923.

The Story of Irving Berlin, with drawings by Neysa McMein.
New York, London, G. P. Putnam's Sons, 1925.

Two Gentlemen and a Lady (*Verdun Belle*), with drawings
by Edwina. New York, Coward-McCann, Inc., 1928.

As You Were, selected by A. Woollcott. New York, The
Viking Press, 1934.

While Rome Burns. New York, The Viking Press, 1934.

The Woollcott Reader; Bypaths in the Realms of Gold, selected by A. Woollcott. New York, The Viking Press, 1935.

Mr. Dickens Goes to the Play. New York, London, G. P. Putnam's Sons, 1922.

ABOUT ALEXANDER WOOLLCOTT:

A. Woollcott, His Life and His World, by Samuel Hopkins Adams. New York, Reynal & Hitchcock, 1945.

Alec the Great, by Philistina (pseudonym). New York, Avalon Press, 1943.

BOOKS ABOUT THE ALGONQUIN HOTEL

Blessed Are the Debonair, by Margaret Case Harriman, with drawings by Mircea. New York, Rinehart, 1956.

Do Not Disturb, by Frank Case; with drawings by O. Soglow. New York, Frederick A. Stokes Co., 1940.

Feeding the Lions; an Algonquin Cookbook, by Frank Case. New York, The Greystone Press, 1942.

Tales of a Wayward Inn, by Frank Case. New York, Frederick A. Stokes Co., 1938.

The Vicious Circle; the Story of the Algonquin Round Table, by Margaret Case Harriman, with drawings by Al Hirschfeld. New York, Rinehart, 1951.